Starting a Business Guide

What Are the Most Practical Industries After the Global Pandemic to Consider for Small and Big Business? In Which Sector, With Which Products, and in What Way Is It Possible to Generate the Highest Revenue? Take Advantage of the Best Business Opportunities Out There Through Detailed Knowledge and Analysis.

Joseph and Julia Mecap

By reading this document, the reader agrees that under no circumstances is the author responsible for any losses, direct or indirect, that are incurred as a result of the use of the information contained within this document, including, but not limited to, errors, omissions, or inaccuracies.

Table of Contents

Introduction..1

    Why Business? 4

Chapter 1 Small Business for Beginners 6

    The Challenges of a Small Business 8

    Examples of Successful Small Businesses.......................21

Chapter 2 Starting and Running a Business After a Pandemic 23

    The Raging Pandemic... 25

Chapter 3 Business Analysis for Beginners...................40

    What Does Business Analysis Entail? 41

    Challenges That Arise Through Business Analysis 45

    Basic Benefits of Business Analysis.............................48

Chapter 4 Developing a Business Plan 50

    Developing A Business Plan...51

Chapter 5 Investing 66

    How to Get Initial Capital 67

    Investing in Your Business..69

    Investing Outside of Your Business............................. 75

Chapter 6 Starting an Online Business 78

Online Business Options 79

The Challenges of Online Business................................83

Online Businesses and the Pandemic............................ 91

Chapter 7 Social Media for Business **94**

Advertising on the Various Platforms 95

Doing Direct Business on Social Media.........................104

Chapter 8 Accounting for Beginners **109**

The Basics of Accounting...109

Taxes 112

Conclusion...**116**

References...**119**

Introduction

The world is full of ideas that were created by somebody who had a vision and the drive to make them become a reality. We can see these visions everywhere we look. Buildings, roads, parks, planes, and various other structures exist because someone or some people had the foresight to create them. They had the ability to look outside the box and create something never done before. It was not easy, but these people had a dream and worked hard to fulfill it. Of course, they had a lot of help along the way, just like anybody else.

If you look within your community, you will see more of these creations in the form of businesses, both big and small. Your local grocery store, your favorite café, the major corporation that hires thousands of employees, the hospital, and even an online store are all business ideas that someone had to come up with. First, they had to think of an idea, and then they had to figure out how they were going to make it work. What did the "making it work" part entail? The finances that would be involved, the necessary resources, a profile of the type of customers the business would be geared toward, the time it would take to build, plans to market the business, and the number of employees needed are just some examples of things that had to be considered.

Once the business was up and running, it was time to make sure it stayed afloat.

It is difficult to run a business in any capacity, and if one is not careful, their dreams can be shattered in an instant. We say this not to deter you but to educate and inform as much as possible. This way, you can be prepared.

This is our personal goal with this book, *Starting a Business Guide*. We want to help you learn about business so that you can create your own someday. Whether it is a big business, small business, or online business, you will be faced with certain challenges, and if you are not prepared, you will fall into the abyss of business owners who never had a shot. While different businesses face different obstacles, they also share some similar ones. The objective here is to figure out what those obstacles will be, dissect them, and then plan how to overcome and even use them to our advantage.

As we go through the various chapters, we will cover many different topics related to business. We will go over the basics of starting a small business, developing a solid plan, looking at business analytics, and marketing yourself and your business properly, among other things. We will also discuss the importance of investing in your business every step of the way so that you can keep it afloat and continue to provide the valuable products and services that you offer.

Amidst the situation that is going on in the year 2020, many businesses are meeting their demise through no fault of their own. While some businesses were going downhill anyway, there is no denying that the current climate pushed them over the edge and did not give them a fighting chance.

Of course, the issue we are speaking of is the Covid-19 pandemic, which has decimated many businesses and industries. This deadly health hazard swept through the world and changed things in an instant. Many businesses were forced to close their doors to help prevent further spread of this virus. Many will never be able to open up again.

Imagine working so hard and putting your blood, sweat, and tears into a business only to have it wiped out by something you could not control. This is a reality for so many people right now, and it is a sad situation to see. While certain measures had to be taken to help save people's lives, there is no denying that businesses were devastated almost overnight.

The reason we said "no fault of their own" earlier is because humanity is facing a catastrophe like nothing else seen in modern times. There was no real way for people to protect their businesses or assets, and as a result, their livelihoods were wiped out. It happened once to so many people, and we don't want it to happen again.

Out of all of the aspects we will discuss, creating a business after a pandemic may be the most imperative. This pandemic has shown us what industries are essential and how businesses can survive and thrive during this economic collapse. It is important to set up a plan to avoid catastrophes, and a raging pandemic is a real threat that we have to deal with now.

Even though times are uncertain, you can still start a business that will appeal to the public and earn you a good income. Of course, much of this goes back to understanding the fundamentals, which we will go over thoroughly in this book.

Why Business?

With all of the challenges that come with starting and running a business, it might be hard for some to understand why this is a path that so many people take. Despite the potential problems and uncertainties, owning a business has many advantages. The one people speak of most highly is having independence from a full-time boss, but there are more. We will delve into those benefits and the various business options that exist. You do not have to be extraordinary in any regard to become a businessperson. However, you have to be willing to do extraordinary things. Even the smallest businesses require sacrifice, which you will learn along the way.

Unfortunately, much of the general public does not understand this sacrifice. They look at many business owners and think they became rich overnight. Much to their surprise, this is rarely, if ever, the case.

Ultimately, we want to make the process as smooth for you as possible. We want you to gain the knowledge you need to make sure your business will become profitable, which is the most important thing. To make a profit, your product or service must be valuable to enough people, and you must make sure the mundane aspects, like finances, are being taken care of properly. Throughout this book, we will cover all of this to make you as prepared as possible.

If you are ready to learn about starting a business and all that it entails, then let's keep moving. Take each chapter one by one, and use the knowledge you gain to achieve real-life success in the business world. As people who have been involved in business and entrepreneurship, we look forward to imparting our knowledge to you.

Chapter 1

Small Business for Beginners

"Freedom is nothing but a chance to be better."

- Albert Camus

Imagine having something you own that is an extension of who you are. You can run it as you please, provide valuable products or services for the public, not worry about a boss, and establish your schedule. This is a dream for many people who work under the authoritarian leadership of a boss for a company they don't want to be a part of. This is a way to gain true freedom. What we are referring to here is the ownership of a business.

There are many different businesses out there, and they all started in the same manner: a dream that someone was able to make a reality. Whether it is a large corporation or a small outfit in the neighborhood, a lot of time, planning, effort, and finances went into establishing it. The goal of this chapter is to focus on small business and how one can be created based on your interests.

Many people look at small business owners and figure they have it made. They go to their little shop, boutique, café, store, or whatever type of establishment they own and don't have to answer to anybody. They have complete autonomy and can run things as they choose. What better way to make an income than running your own small business?

Let's put the brakes on for a minute. We certainly do not want to impede your desire to run a business, but we also do not want you to go in blind without the proper preparation. Many factors go into creating a small business. Much to the dismay of many, you cannot just take over a location anywhere and start selling whatever your business does. Before you even consider this phase of opening, you must go through several other steps first so your grand opening will be smooth and without much delay.

Once you open the doors, that's when the real fun starts. It is now time to keep the business afloat, which may be even more challenging than opening in the first place. As we go through this chapter, we will cover the many different facets to consider when starting up and running a small business.

Owning a business can be a great experience where you get to serve the public in a manner that is different from working a regular job. You get to put your heart and soul into something that will become an extension of you and your interests. If everything goes well, you can even make a great profit.

While we are not going to tell you what type of business to open, the information we provide will be foundational across the board in most industries. Whatever type of business you own, certain measures must be addressed and taken care of. Never assume that a business will take off automatically based simply on public opinion. There are many variables to consider if starting a profitable business that stays consistent throughout the years. We will delve into these various factors now to get you fully informed about starting a small business.

The Challenges of a Small Business

There are millions of small businesses in the United States in many different industries. The criterion for a small business is generally dependent on the number of employees or wages earned per year. Many consider these operations to be the local mini-marts, flower shops, and restaurants along the city streets. These locations fall under the small business umbrella, but they do not encompass all of the various types that exist.

Depending on the industry, a small business can be defined as having a maximum of 250 employees or up to 1,500, which may sound ridiculous to even consider. The definition may also depend on the amount of revenue the company takes in per year, which is also based on industry.

The Small Business Administration, or SBA, has specific standards set for a company to fall within the limits of a small business. The SBA covers many different sectors, but here are a few to give you an idea:

- Finance and Insurance: A maximum of 1,500 employees and average earnings between $32.5 million and $38.5 million.
- Real Estate, Rental, and Leasing: Based on maximum earnings between $7.5 million and $32.5 million.
- Transportation and Warehousing: A range of employees between 500 and 1,500 and earnings between $7.5 million and $37.5 million.

There are many other industries with their own criteria, and you can find an SBA table of size standards online for specific information (McIntyre, 2017). We just want to give you a few examples of what constitutes a small business. The good news is that you will have many different options to choose from when figuring out what type of small business you want to run. Look at the various industries and determine which one you are most interested in. For example, if you grew up on a ranch or farm, you may be interested in agriculture. Of course, we are just assuming here.

You will also need to consider whether you want sole proprietorship, where you work alone, or want to have employees. Each option comes with its set of challenges. With the sole proprietorship, you will have much more freedom and responsibility since there is no one else to look out for businesswise. Of course, this will limit you on how many products and services you can offer due to limited hands on deck. For example, if you work in landscaping, you will only be able to do one house at a time, whereas if you have employees, you can cover many different areas at once.

Being the only employee in the business plus the owner means that you will need to be on the front line and do all the dirty work, like accounting, taxes, inventory, bookkeeping, and marketing. All of these responsibilities may wear you out and keep you from providing the services to your customers.

If you plan on having employees, you will have many extra hands to perform the duties of the business. You will also have other things to worry about, like benefits, payroll, liability insurance, and employees who are competent and give good customer service. Remember that your employees reflect you and your business, so it is in your favor to do some proper vetting. Many organizations are satisfied with warm bodies in whatever capacity. However, if these bodies are doing nothing, then it is pointless to have them, and you are just bleeding money. These are just a few things to consider. Let's go over several other aspects of starting and running a small business.

Before Opening Your Doors

Before you even open the doors to your business, whatever it may be, you will have to do some heavy preparation and research. It can be overwhelming, but these steps cannot be avoided if you want your business to run as smoothly as possible. It goes well beyond just providing a product or service that people want. There are numerous factors to consider before deciding if it will be worth it to move forward. Unfortunately, many people do miss some crucial steps, either because they were not aware or did not have the patience. This is why so many small businesses fail.

According to Forbes, about 20% of small businesses fail in the first year. About 50% fail within five years. Beyond this, only about ⅓ of businesses make it to the 10-year mark. This is a staggering number of businesses that fail. With the recent pandemic, many more businesses have become casualties. We will get more into that in the next chapter but realize that it's not just a matter of working hard. There are plenty of hardworking people who failed miserably. It is about making the right choices and working efficiently. We are not saying any of this to scare you. We just want to set you up for success. Owning your own business can be a wonderful thing, but you must do it the right way.

The first step is to decide you want to open a business. Next, do some thorough research about the industry you want to get involved in.

Will you be able to dominate with your idea, or is the market too saturated already? For example, if you plan on opening a coffee shop, are there several in your town already? If so, what will make yours unique? How will you compete with these established outfits, especially the big companies?

You must also consider your target demographic. Who will be the target customers, and are there enough in the area? Also, the customer range as far as distance should be looked into. As a business, you need to deliver on what your clientele wants; otherwise, you will have no one to sell to.

The legal aspects should also be looked into. It is important to choose a legal structure. This will help determine the proper paperwork, taxes, and liability of the owner. There are several options, like LLC, DBA, or corporation. When opening a business, you want to make sure you are as protected as possible, so you must also look into getting the proper licenses and obtaining an employer identification number based on the regulations of your state. Legalzoom.com is a good website to get more legal information from. You can also consult with an attorney if needed but try Legal Zoom or a similar website first.

Next, you will have to map your finances. Most people starting businesses do not have a nest egg or endless cash resources. They must develop a plan to obtain capital so they can have the money needed to open their business. A common approach is borrowing from friends or family and then paying them back. The individual parties can decide if interest will be involved. The next option is getting a business loan from a bank or credit union. If you believe in your idea enough and other people do too, then you can also seek out a venture capitalist or angel investor. Finally, saving up enough of your own capital through various sources of income can be done too. This may take a while, and it's important to get your business up and going. Only go this route if you have no other options. Maintain strict records of your expenses. You will need them for tax purposes.

Timing is an important element when starting up a business. First, consider what the economy is like and whether it is healthy enough to build a new business. Are the people in your community working and bringing in an income? If not, they probably won't have the income to buy whatever you're selling.

Also, creating a business takes some decisiveness. Do not dwell on a decision for so long that you end up not doing it. The longer you have to think about something, the less likely it is to get done. We are not telling you to go in blindly. But once you've done your research and are fairly sure you want to go through with it, then go for it. You may never obtain 100% certainty, but you don't have to in order to make a good decision.

It is tempting to try and do everything yourself when starting a business, especially when you have little money. It is not a smart move, though, because it will be quite an undertaking. Unless you plan on going into business with a friend or family member who can ease the burden, you should consider hiring someone to help you with the legwork. For example, an accountant is essential to keep track of your expenses and income. They will also be able to help with your taxes, which will be a huge benefit. You want to focus as much as you can on the actual product or service you will be selling. This is difficult when you have so many distractions.

Find help for the complicated stuff that you do not know anything about. This will free up your time so you can focus on the important aspects of your business, like the customers. Of course, do your research and find a reliable person. It is easy to look someone up online and get reviews of past work.

Finally, you must consider the risk factor. There is always a certain level of risk in starting a business, and if you are not okay with that, then it's better to not start at all. The important thing is to take calculated risks and cover as many of your bases as possible. This is why we went over all of the previous steps. Going through all of them will minimize risk, and then you have to take a leap of faith.

There are also specific risks associated with particular industries. For example, healthcare, real estate, and finance sectors may require you to get personal liability insurance to protect your assets in case of a lawsuit.

Coming Up with Unique Business Ideas

A small business does not have to be isolated to whatever you see on the streets or in communities. There are many creative ideas that people have had and created businesses from. In most cases, it was an extension of something that interested them. From their creative minds, they had a great thought and turned it into a moneymaker. Or maybe they saw a problem that needed to be solved, so they fixed it. You can do the same thing.

One of the great things about a small business is that it does not have to have a large initial investment. In many cases, people can start one out of their home. Of course, depending on where you live, you may need to research the specific regulations, so you are not breaking any rules. We always advise that you stay within the confines of legal guidelines or all of your hard work can be gone in an instant.

We want to help you come up with a creative business idea of your own. Of course, we do not know you, so we will not be getting specific here. We just want to provide a general overview of how you can come up with a money-making pathway by doing something that's already a part of your life. The following are a few steps you can take to come up with the next great business idea that helps people in some way:

Think about what's coming up next. What are some innovations being done in society, and how can you get in on the action? For example, will people be looking to technologically upgrade their homes?

What are some issues in your life related to inconvenience? If you are struggling with them, other people might be too.

Are there more cost-effective ways to do something? Can this be a benefit to other people?

Colin Barceloux was once a student who thought textbooks cost way too much. Instead of just griping, he did something about it. Two years after graduating, he founded Bookrenter.com in San Mateo, California, which allows textbook rentals at a 60% discount. It now has over 1.5 million users.

Look for new niches that are big at the moment. Look at what is missing in a big industry and see if you can fill the void somehow.

What particular skills do you have, and how can they be utilized to provide specific products and services? This can even be a hobby-turned-business idea.

An example of this was when people who had sewing skills were able to create and sell masks for people to use. If you are not good at sewing, consider your other skill sets and interests, like art, pottery, and cleaning homes. Many people are great at organizing and generate income organizing people's homes and offices.

What skills or training do you have that can help you transition into having another source of income? For example, if you are a teacher, you may be able to start tutoring. If you work in healthcare, you can teach people CPR. If you are great at a musical instrument, you can start giving private lessons.

Many different creative business ideas are out there. You just have to look outside the box. Many people out there do these small businesses right out of their home, and if you know someone who does, pick their brain.

Potential Complications While Running a Business

Once you have your small business up and running, it is an exciting time. There is a certain joy that comes with owning something, and having your business is a wonderful feeling. Don't let this excitement make you comfortable, though. The real work is just beginning. You must remain focused on all aspects of your business or you will run into trouble. Do not ignore the smaller things like unnecessary expenditures. These will add up and eventually sink your business. At the least, they will reduce your profit margins, and you deserve to keep as much of your money as you can.

Money management is one of the biggest problems for people running a business. You must keep track of all your expenditures and also maintain proper cash flow. If you are not bringing money in, then there's no point in running the business. If you are bringing in a steady income, your revenue will still likely be down if your money management skills are not good. Numerous online applications and programs can help you keep track of expenses and income, create invoices, and keep your stuff organized if you ever need to access it in the future. We will discuss accounting more in a later chapter.

Another major problem is inadequate marketing. Marketing is a tough game because it is how you get customers in the first place. There are so many marketing strategies out there, and some can cost an arm and a leg. What is worse is that you have no idea if it will work or not. Marketing comes in all shapes and sizes. The old-school method of word-of-mouth still works great. This is when a satisfied customer leaves a positive review, which will engage other customers.

Let people know about your business, and make sure you have an online presence. Even if you don't run an online business, you still need to be online in some way. You can create a website, use social media, or both. Offline techniques like ads in newspapers, flyers, business cards, and billboards are acceptable too. You don't have to break the bank with marketing, though.

Marketing is a great way to get customers, but to retain them, you have to provide good business. Customers stay when they are taken care of. Yes, price and how much they can save is important. However, if they are getting more than their money's worth, they will be a happy customer and return regularly. Customers must feel like they're important and never a burden. If you treat them this way, they will go somewhere else.

"A customer is the most important visitor on our premises. He is not dependent on us. We are dependent on him. He is not an interruption in our work. He is the purpose of it. He is not an outsider in our business. He is part of it. We are not doing him a favor by serving him. He is doing us a favor by giving us an opportunity to do so."

- Mahatma Gandhi

There are only so many hours in a day, and it is important to use them wisely. You must be productive and manage your time well to complete everything you need to. Set up your schedule for the next day the night before and stick to it as much as possible. Account for delays where possible. Always do the most important tasks first so that if something needs to wait, it is of less importance. Finally, delegate where you can. This is where hiring people to do things like taxes and accounting can come in handy so that you can focus on other aspects of your business. Poor time management will lead to important areas of your business getting neglected.

Never forget why you started your business. You wanted to provide a product or service you believed in and make a great income doing so. Always focus on the business at hand and make sure customer satisfaction is your goal, as cliché as that may sound.

Getting Business Advice

Here's a question to consider. If you wanted to travel to a specific location, who would you ask? Who is likely to give you great advice? Probably, someone who has lived there or has traveled there before. If you wanted advice on cooking, you would ask someone who is a good cook. If you wanted to become a lawyer, you would get advice from a lawyer. Why is it, then, when people want to start a business, they ask their friends or family who have never started a business before? Those who are close to you may have your best interests at heart, but they may not be able to give you sound advice because they will either be too kind or too critical.

Just like any other field, it is best to get guidance from a business owner who is currently where you want to be. There are many great ways to connect with fellow business owners, like online clubs or even in-person clubs. Networking is also a great way to get known and learn. Sites like meetup.com are great ways to find business clubs to be a part of. Also, look out for business and networking events in your area. Learn from great minds wherever you can find them.

Examples of Successful Small Businesses

Out of the small businesses that do make it, most of them remain small. They certainly grow and gain customers, but they do not leave any major mark. However, some of these minute ventures turn into something huge and practically take over the world. We are willing to bet that you utilize some of these companies in your own life. The following are a few companies that started as small operations but eventually became juggernauts in their own right:

- Facebook: Facebook was started as a small website in a dorm room at Harvard by Mark Zuckerberg. It was a way for college students to share ideas and information. It is now worth hundreds of billions of dollars, roughly $350 billion as of 2016.

- Amazon: This company was started by Jeff Bezos in his garage. At first, it was just an online retailer for shipping books. Now, you can get almost anything from Amazon, and it is hard to imagine a time where online shipping did not exist. Amazon is currently the most valuable company in the world, and Jeff Bezos is the richest man by far. Some people believe he may become the world's first trillionaire.

- YouTube: You can find almost any type of video on YouTube now. It is worth billions of dollars, but it started as a small idea in a cubicle. Two friends, Chad Hurley and Steven Chen, wanted a simpler way to share videos with friends online. That little idea became this massive content juggernaut.

- Mattel: This massive toy company was started by a Polish immigrant, Ruth Handler, and her husband, Elliot. They did not have business experience or capital. They just had a great idea and believed in themselves.

We are not saying you will end up becoming one of these powerhouses. We are just showing you the potential that exists. If you play your cards right, you can create a great business that will serve you and others well.

Chapter 2

Starting and Running a Business After a Pandemic

Imagine running your business, and everything is going great. You have a great product that people love, and it is generating great income. You have customers backed up for days because they love what you are selling so much. Suddenly, you get hit with something unexpected, and it throws you completely off course. It depletes your business out of nowhere and forces you to lose your customers. Eventually, you have to close down shop permanently, through no fault of your own.

The story seems unfathomable, but it has occurred. Unfortunately, the world was recently hit by a deadly pandemic that affected millions of lives. Considering it spread across the globe, you could even say it affected billions of people. Millions of people either lost their lives or came close as this health crisis ravaged the globe. Due to the many precautions that had to be taken to prevent further spread, everyone's life had to be altered greatly, which meant businesses could not run as before. Many had to alter their practices significantly, while others had to shut their doors until further notice.

Many businesses were able to make adjustments, mainly by utilizing new technology and services that were available. For example, many restaurants got rid of physical menus and developed a way for customers to download menus by using the cameras on their smartphones to hover over a scanner. Many restaurants also utilized delivery services like Door Dash or Uber Eats more often. The bottom line is that these businesses were able to figure out a way to survive.

Several businesses were not able to open up again, either because they weren't allowed to or could not afford to stay afloat with all of the changes. Unfortunately, many of these were the small businesses we discussed in the previous chapter. Of course, large corporations did not go unscathed, and many of them had to close a large percentage of their stores. Regardless of size, there has been a lot of debate on how to save those businesses that went under so quickly.

What cannot be debated is that they were hit with something unexpected and well beyond their control. The damage that was done is done, and the best thing to do is recover the best we can and learn from the past. The focus of this chapter will be about starting a business after a pandemic. We live in a different world from the past, and issues that happen abroad can affect us here. When we consider potential problems, we must think on a global scale to a certain degree.

The Raging Pandemic

While the many deaths and illnesses caused by the recent pandemic are the worst results to come out of it, the many people who lost their livelihoods, savings, and homes are also terrible tragedies. We are not going to get into politics or start finger-pointing here. The focus will be on creating a business that can survive after the pandemic. To do this, we will assess how to start and run the business, so it succeeds in the long run. Even if there was never a pandemic and we are lucky enough to not get another one soon, there are always things that can threaten your business from the inside and out. It is best to be as prepared as possible for anything that can potentially harm your business.

Why Were Businesses Impacted?

Businesses were impacted because people were asked to stay home and many businesses were asked to shut their doors for a short-term period until the experts were able to figure everything out. The initial two weeks were not that big of a problem, and if everything could have opened up by then, not too much harm would have been done. At most, businesses would have had some catching up to do. Unfortunately, this was not the end. After two weeks, people were still asked to stay at home, and businesses had to make several changes if they wanted to keep their doors open.

People were still terrified of the deadly virus, and even when they were allowed inside businesses at a limited capacity, they did not feel comfortable doing so. Most businesses were not able to open up to full capacity due to the limitations they had to follow. Some businesses also had to change their practices to allow for better infection control and safety for the population. While some businesses survived for a little while, others never opened back up again. Some businesses are just barely holding on, and the future looks bleak if they do not follow guidelines and adapt quickly.

Many businesses have survived and thrived, though. This is because they were able to adapt quickly or had a great business model before the pandemic that protected them from any major threat. While some of the businesses closed because their particular product or service had no chance of surviving no matter what, others were going downhill already, and the pandemic just pushed them over the edge.

According to the Bureau of Labor Statistics, the industries hit hardest by the pandemic were airlines, gambling, hotels, movie theaters, live sporting events, restaurants, retail, shipping, and film production, just to name a few. You may look at something like airlines and think that's not a small business. While that's true, they can affect small businesses with interruptions in shipping and traveling. Also, many connected businesses, like independent travel agencies, will feel the pinch.

Economists currently estimate that over 100,000 small businesses have closed in the United States alone. This is a devastating number as these types of businesses have upheld the economy for decades.

Businesses are continuing to adapt as needed based on new regulations coming out. However, we are not out of the woods at this moment in 2020, and there is a major chance of resurgence, which may create even greater problems than there already are.

Unfortunately, this fear of going out will not let up anytime soon, even with all of the new regulations being made. Business owners are taking a huge hit because people continue to be afraid or annoyed by everything going on. There is still a lot of uncertainty with the pandemic, which makes matters even worse.

It is hard to pinpoint any other event in modern times that had such a significant global impact as Covid-19. Almost everyone on the planet was affected in some way.

How Did Businesses Survive?

Our focus is to look at businesses that survived and succeeded during the pandemic. What did they do right that we can learn from? Many companies were forced to look at their structure and determine where the major holes were. We mentioned before that some businesses were already on the downward swing before the pandemic. They either had poor business practices beforehand or were part of a dying industry. There are reasons, though, that some businesses survived the pandemic and are continuing to perform well. There are also reasons why people are still able to open a business now, even though it may sound like the most ridiculous time to do so.

First, companies that had a digital presence remained strong even during the darkest times. At the height of the pandemic, many organizations were forced to transition to remote work as soon as possible. Of course, major bumps arose when customers did not have the knowledge or technology to access services or products online. In addition, many employees needed to be retrained so they could work remotely. Companies that already had an online presence and did most of their work remotely had an obvious head start. Others had to hustle to catch up. Amazon and Facebook are the prototypes here of providing great digital service; however, they are hardly small businesses.

Sectors like the financial service, wealth management, retail, and various other professional services were heavily lacking in their online presence. The bottom line is that if you want your small business to survive right now, do as much work as you can digitally. Even restaurants and retail are following this trend. It has never been easier to order something online and have it delivered to your house or pick it up quickly at the curb.

Speaking of this, curbside pickup was another area that grew significantly. People were able to search for their products online, order them, and then pick them up directly from the businesses where an employee was waiting for them. These businesses were industrious and used the resources they had available to their advantage.

Small businesses had no choice but to make the necessary alterations based on the new regulations coming in. Social distancing, proper sanitation practices, a limited number of customers in a store, and employees wearing masks were just some of the new practices being put in place. Beyond these new guidelines, all of the methods we described before, like proper marketing, money management, and great customer service, are essential. It has been challenging, and there are no easy answers. However, it is not impossible. Your small business can still survive after a pandemic, just as so many have.

For those of you shouting and saying that it's not fair for businesses to have to go through this, we agree with you. That does not change reality, though. Unfortunately, life is not fair in many aspects, but this cannot stop you from moving forward. We know the pandemic caused a lot of havoc, but if it wasn't that, it would have been something else that threatened your business. Maybe not to the same extreme, but these threats would have still been present.

Let's take a look at some businesses that exemplified strength, versatility, grit, and intelligence and did what needed to be done to keep their doors open. Despite the pandemic, these businesses flourished.

For this section, we will focus on several businesses out of the Baltimore area, which is a major metro area that suffered tremendously under the Covid-19 crisis. When the governor of Maryland issued a stay-at-home order, it was the death knell for many small businesses. There were a select few, though, that overcame the issues and are doing better than ever. Their stories mirror many other victories that people have had all over the country.

Benson Watch Co.:

Marcel Benson is the owner of Benson Watch Co., and like so many other small business owners, he was worried that his company would not survive the pandemic. Before the crisis, his company was approaching about $1 million in sales, according to *Black Enterprise*. Once the pandemic reared its ugly head, Benson watched numerous businesses around him cutting costs in every way. This included marketing and advertising. The last thing people wanted to do was put money into ads when they were barely able to pay their bills.

Benson could have followed suit here. If people are panicking over something, others will react and follow their lead. This was not the case for Benson, though. Instead, he ramped up his marketing by investing in ads on Facebook and Instagram. This gave Benson Watch Co. continued exposure, while other companies were slowly disappearing into the abyss. As a result, sales quadrupled, and the business is doing better than ever. Benson did not let fear overtake him. He went against the grain and did the opposite of what so many in his position were doing.

Marketing is one of the most significant factors in running a business. Without it, nobody will know that you exist, no matter how great your product or service is. Marcel Benson knew this and acted accordingly. "We learned in, and we put a little more into our budget, and it turned out that it paid a lot more than it would have prior," Benson stated (Wilen, 2020).

Wight Tea Co.:

Started by the sister-brother duo Brittney and Joe Wight, Wight Tea Co. has mainly operated as a wholesale tea seller since its inception in 2016. Their products consist of loose-leaf teas, small-batch tea blends, and brewed teas on the go. The plan this year was to open a stall at the popular Whitehall Market in Baltimore, which was newly renovated. This would allow their products to have more visibility and direct sales to the public. When Covid-19 hit, it put an immediate stop to their plan, as many companies were forced to operate through delivery or carry-out services. Wight Tea Co. also lost their wholesale orders.

Like so many businesses, Wight Tea Co. could have been run into the ground and forced to close their doors. They were panicking when they lost all of their sources of income, and who could blame them. However, Brittney and Joe Wight played their cards correctly, and as a result, they thrived like never before. Similar to Benson, Brittney and Joe tapped into digital marketing. Their direct-to-customer sales increased immensely due to their website. They have also received some of their wholesale business back by working with a concierge service located in Washington D.C. This service was delivering care packages to office workers, and Wight Tea Co. was delivering about 200 tons per month during the height of the shutdown.

Brittney and Joe Wight are still moving forward with their plan to open a stall at Whitehall Market. They said that the delay was a blessing in disguise as it gave them more time to prepare for a physical store. This sister-brother team showed that you need to be innovative and ready to change course as needed to survive.

Motown Fermentation:

This juice shop was founded in Hampden, Maryland, in 2015. At the height of its growth, it became one of Maryland's most successful businesses with products in more than a thousand stores across nine states. Due to the extreme growth, the company opened a 13,000 square-foot brewery in Northwest Baltimore.

Unfortunately, the pandemic hit, which threatened Motown Fermentation's success. Nine employees had to be let go despite the business getting a Paycheck Protection Program loan and various other forms of financial assistance. With all of its restaurant and cafe partners being shut down, Motown had to adapt quickly. The founder, Sid Sharma, stated that the company had to rely on customers at grocery stores for cash revenue. The company began doing more home deliveries as well. This proved convenient for their customers.

Motown has been able to stay afloat and prosper. They still have many partnerships in the making and are expected to come back stronger than ever.

These businesses are great examples of what someone needs to do following a major threat like the Covid-19 pandemic. They were able to adapt quickly and continue to follow the foundational techniques of maintaining a business. The health crisis could have destroyed them as well. However, their swift action prevented this from happening. If you plan on starting a business either during or after the pandemic, then these companies and their owners showcased some great practices to model yourself after.

The Best Businesses to Start

The recent pandemic brought to light the many holes that businesses have in their ability to deal with emergencies. While this was an exceptional case, it can still teach us a lot about starting and running a business properly. One of the challenges is finding businesses or industries that are most likely to survive a pandemic. In this section, we will discuss some excellent business ideas for you to consider that will continue to bring in revenue even if people are not living their lives as they used to. The following are some business ideas that will not only survive the pandemic but may become greater opportunities for entrepreneurs than ever before.

Cleaning and Janitorial Services:

One thing that was exposed during the Covid-19 scare was the lack of cleanliness and sanitation in our homes, workplaces, and environment in general. This new revelation has made the demand for janitorial and cleaning services rise exponentially. Many different businesses are searching for good companies that can help keep their workplace settings clean and healthy for their employees. People share many common areas, and this is how many illnesses spread. Having a good cleaning service can gain you a lot of traction and provide a great revenue stream. After the pandemic is over, this demand for cleanliness will remain as many organizations will need to keep up with health guidelines according to government agencies.

One of the easiest ways to get into this industry is to become involved with an existing company that already has name recognition. You can then get training with their products and equipment and become an independent contractor for them.

Stylish Face Coverings:

We spoke earlier about the need for masks during the pandemic and how many entrepreneurs are already jumping on this bandwagon. If you can sew, then this opportunity may be right up your alley. If you can make 10 to 20 face masks in a day and sell them all, then you can make a pretty good profit. If you do not know how to sew, some companies can make the masks and sell them to you wholesale. You can even request a specific logo on the masks. Another option is to seek out a friend who can sew and then allow them to manage the labor while you take care of the business practices. It can get tricky working with someone, so be careful.

E-Commerce:

This may become one of, if not the most, profitable business sectors for continued profit. With many physical stores receiving the death blow during the pandemic, online stores have seen an explosion in sales. Many new niches have popped up over the last few months, and e-commerce has never looked back since it started growing. You can start your online store or get connected through companies like Amazon or eBay. Shopify is a great way to participate in drop shipping, where you don't even have to carry your inventory. You simply act as the middleman between the supplier and the customer. Pay attention to the fees as they will cut into your profit margins.

Freelance Work and Side Hustles:

Freelance work is when you offer your services based on your skills and abilities. For example, if you are well versed with a piano, you can give private lessons. If you enjoy manual labor, you can offer to mow people's lawns. If you are in healthcare, you can get your CPR instructor's certification and begin teaching classes. Think about your skills and what you can offer to the public.

The great thing about freelance work and side hustles is that you can do it on your own time. Many people begin by working on their days off from their regular jobs. Some individuals can build their clientele and start bringing in a full-time income. The key here is to have all of the foundational business skills, like marketing, money management, and customer service, present. Also, you must stand by your work and be able to back up your talk.

Keeping track of your finances is essential for side hustles and freelance gigs. Many people neglect to disclose their income from these various jobs that they perform. This will create many issues in the long run. If the IRS ever finds out that you are withholding earned income from them, then an audit is a major possibility.

Classic Businesses:

It is still possible to run a classic brick-and-mortar style business. Many people are still doing it and succeeding like never before. We provided some great examples in the previous section. Again, the key is to have all of the basic business practices covered and pay attention to what societal demands are at the time. No matter what type of business you run, an online presence is essential.

Financial Relief for Small Businesses

The bottom line is that a business needs to make money to survive. It is how the owner pays their bills, including payroll for the employees. Also, money needs to be reinvested into the company to help it grow and prosper. The main issue during Covid-19 was businesses trying to get some financial relief after their profits took a nosedive. The stimulus checks offered by the government were not nearly enough to keep everything afloat.

Business owners have to search for several resources to help them out financially. The following are a few ideas for businesses to go to in order to seek out additional aid and relief until they can get back on their feet. If you are planning to pursue these ideas, whether starting or already running a business, remember that they are short-term aids and not meant to be permanent solutions.

- Coronavirus small business administration loans: These loans by the SBA offer assistance to small businesses that are unable to find credit elsewhere. Their interest rates are low, at 3.75%, and repayment plans are up to 30 years.

- Leniency from credit card companies: Many credit card companies will be offering relief for small businesses. Various efforts are being made, which includes waving service fees for 30 days. Check with your own credit card companies to see what they offer.
- State and local resources are available based on the area that you live in. Your best resource here is your local chamber of commerce.
- Crowdfunding through online fundraisers is a great way for customers to show extra support for the businesses they enjoy frequenting. Crowdfunding revenue can be used for things like health insurance for employees, monthly rent or mortgage, employee assistance programs, employee crisis pay, and various other business expenses.
- Federal assistance: The Payment Protection Program, which was rolled out by the federal government, aims to help businesses keep current employees on the payroll. Businesses with fewer than 500 employees can receive up to 2.5 times their monthly payroll in loans, with an interest rate of 1%.

These are just a few options for small businesses to help them stay above water during the pandemic. Even the best businesses need assistance during this time, so do not hesitate to seek out these programs if you need them (*Coronavirus Relief for Small Businesses: Seven Ways to Get Help*, 2020).

The main takeaway from this chapter is that most businesses have suffered and will continue to be affected by the pandemic. While certain industries are more disaster-proof than others, how you manage your business from start to finish is more imperative than the type of business.

Chapter 3

Business Analysis for Beginners

You may have heard the phrase, "The smallest hole will ultimately sink the biggest ship." This metaphor correlates directly to managing a business, no matter how big or small. While looking at the larger picture, many business owners ignore the obvious threats that have the potential to take down an organization. Many great companies of the past went down because they ignored significant warning signs that were causing great issues. By the time they noticed or paid attention, it was too late for intervention.

Knowing business analysis allows us to monitor and identify the needs of an organization and determine the best solutions to solve problems, both real and potential. Changes that arise through proper analysis can include things like process improvement, organizational change, strategic planning, or policy development. These are the essentials to help avoid major gaps in business practices, keeping the small holes in the ship concealed.

Businesses that do not change never grow. They also get ignored and eventually fall apart. Business analysis will help you do business better, period. This field covers many different sectors within a business and can assist with change and development at any level. This practice will be especially useful in helping companies progress through unchartered territories, like the pandemic in Chapter 2.

We will cover the different areas of business analysis to illustrate the benefits it provides. With proper analysis, you will save on unnecessary business costs, identify new opportunities for growth, assess ways in which a business must change to keep up with the times, and determine what potential setbacks might exist.

What Does Business Analysis Entail?

Business analysis is a discipline that uses in-depth research to identify the needs of a business and determine the most comprehensive solutions to a business problem. It is a set of tasks that connects stakeholders with a business to help them understand the organization's structure, policies, and operations. Stakeholders are important because, without their financial backing, a company would cease to exist. This is why business analysis is so crucial. Even the most successful businesses in the world have issues that arise, so regular analysis is a necessity to catch any of these issues before they become more serious than they need to be. To be a good business analyst, you must understand how your organization functions to fulfill its purpose. The following are some critical steps for a proper business analysis process.

Getting Oriented:

Of course, the first step in the process is to get clarification of the scope, requirements, and objectives of the business. A collection of some basic information will be done during this time. If a business analyst is already within an organization, then this step may take less time than if you hired an outside contractor. During this step, the main responsibilities are:

- Determining the primary stakeholders and who they are.
- Having an understanding of the business and project history.
- Understanding the system of the business and its processes.

Basically, the business analyst will understand the business well before they proceed.

Identify the Business's Primary Objective:

In this step, the business's needs will be identified. Proper analysis will confirm the expectations of the shareholders and also merge conflicting expectations. This step in the process will ensure the business objectives are clear and reasonable, meaning they are attainable based on the current system. These objectives must also set the stage for the business scope.

Define the Scope:

The scope is not an actual implementation plan. It will simply guide all of the steps in the business analysis process. This will help the team understand the business's needs to move forward. The role of the business analyst will be to:

- Define a solution method to recognize what technology and process changes need to be made.
- Review the project/business objectives with the stakeholders.
- Look at the justification and benefits of a business's project or undertaking.

Create the Business Analysis Plan:

This step will provide clarity to the business analysis process. It will answer any questions from those involved with the project or business at hand. During the business analysis plan process, the vital responsibilities will be:

- Deciding the most appropriate deliverables that can be provided during business analysis.
- Defining the specific list of deliverables or benefits to be provided. The specific stakeholders should be identified.
- Providing a good timeline for when the deliverables can be finished.

Basically, what are the benefits that will come from the business analysis plan?

Define the Requirements:

Detailed requirements that are actionable must be provided to the implementation team so they have accurate and adequate information to devise a proper solution. During this step, the business analyst will:

- Collect necessary information and analyze it to create a first-draft report.
- Review and confirm the deliverables and make sure they are reasonable and can be provided.
- Ask accurate questions to fill any gaps in the plan.

Provide Support for the Technical Implementation:

The implementation team will now build, customize, and deploy the necessary software. The role of the business analyst will be to:

- Review the final solution design.
- Assist the quality assurance professionals and ensure they understand the importance of the technical requirements.
- Be there as a backup to answer any last-minute questions.

Help the Solution Be Applied:

The business analyst will be involved in this final step to support the business in case they are not able to use the solutions properly. This way, the original objectives are more likely to be met. This step will help ensure that all members involved are ready for the changes that will come from implementing the solutions.

Assess the Value Created by the Solution:

There are many steps in the business analysis process, and many analysts lose track of what the objectives and benefits are. In this final step, it is time to assess the value created by the solutions. The business analyst will:

- Evaluate the progress achieved through the process.
- Relay the results to the project sponsor and other team members. Everyone who needs to know should be filled in.

The expected benefit of this process is that the business will grow and have more opportunities. If a business is constantly being kept from reaching its potential due to setbacks, then those need to be addressed.

Challenges That Arise Through Business Analysis

Business analysts are required to be great communicators and facilitators so they can relay massive amounts of information to the technical team. This is an extremely vital role because if no one is aware of the issues, they will not be solved. While business analysts are skilled individuals, they are just human in the end. Many problems arise that make their job difficult to handle. We will go over some of these problems and the solutions.

Paralysis by Analysis:

This term relates to taking in massive amounts of information that you have to process in a short period. This crunch can cause a person to become overwhelmed. This issue generally arises when an analyst does not know where to start and stop with their process. Overanalyzing is caused by:

- Asking questions repeatedly to get clarification.
- Seeking to confirm requirements over and over again without any gain or progress.
- Developing more models than required.
- Stretching the analysis phase instead of coming closer to the desired result.

To combat this problem, the analysis process should seek to solve a few issues at a time and move forward rather than taking care of everything at once and extending the whole process. Any unnecessary information should be filtered out, and the process should only focus on relevant information that is needed to produce a solution.

Limited Knowledge and Skills:

Business analysts are in a unique position where they must understand the business and technical aspects of an organization. These are two vastly different fields that require a lot of knowledge. When analysts focus on one aspect and not the other, it will be detrimental to the process as a whole. The business analyst is always on a learning curve.

From day one, the business analyst should learn everything they can about the business, industry, and available technology. Having focused knowledge and training in certain areas can increase the command a person has of a specific area. If you have a business with employees, never transition any of them into this role without proper training. They need to be cultivated well so they are nurtured for the role.

Power:

Because of their skills and knowledge, business analysts have a lot of influence over business and project decisions. It can be difficult to be objective and do what's best for the company rather than what's best for the analyst. Analysts can become a barrier between the business and technical side rather than a bridge.

Business analysts must remain aware of what is right and wrong. Any decision that is made should be made available to the stakeholders, and the reasons behind these decisions have to be transparent. The stakeholder has to be treated fairly and not deceived in any way. If you need to hire a business analyst, then do your research ahead of time to get the most reliable person.

Uncooperative Stakeholders:

Business analysts will often deal with uncooperative stakeholders who refuse to disclose a variety of important information. They often withhold information out of fear, worry, disgust, disinterest, or being self-conscious. Be mindful of this if your analyst is facing this issue.

A good analyst will know how to circumnavigate this issue and get the information they need. They will not take it personally. For example, if a stakeholder is not upfront about information, the analyst can request documents that must be handed over to them and retrieve the information from there.

Basic Benefits of Business Analysis

While business analysis is a lengthy and in-depth process, it can provide your organization with a lot of value. Just like any other skilled professional that can help run your business, hiring a business analyst should be considered carefully. The following are some of the benefits of doing so:

- The company will hemorrhage less money.
- Increased ROI in the future. With finding ways to reduce cost, increase revenue, and improve investment strategies, your overall company value will increase, along with the ROI.
- There will be many more successful projects and home runs for the company.
- Better collaboration with stakeholders, which will require less rework on projects.

When working with a business analyst, provide them with the information they need. The better you work with them, the more effective the process will be.

If you found this book to be valuable, then please help other people learn about it by leaving a review.

Chapter 4

Developing a Business Plan

Imagine for a moment that you are a contractor. You start putting down the foundation of the house, and then you begin building it from the ground up with various materials. In the end, the structure of the house is misshaped, and several pieces are missing. Furthermore, the house does not look steady because of the poor foundation. Why did the house turn out this way? Because you, the contractor, had no plan and just started building. As a result, you created a house that no one would live in.

It may seem ludicrous to build a home without a blueprint, and it is. What is equally ridiculous is starting a business without having an actual plan in place. Yet, many people are guilty of doing the latter, which is a major reason their businesses fall apart, despite how good their products and services are.

A solid business plan is essential and must take into account many different factors. These include:

- Your current situation regarding finances, resources, knowledge, and training.
- Current and potential obstacles that may arise.
- A good contingency plans.
- How the business will be built and structured. For example, will you take over an existing location or find a new one?

If you are planning on starting a business soon, no matter what kind it is, make sure you have a good business plan. If you have not created one yet, then we suggest you stop and do so. In the next section, we will help you come up with a business plan that fits your particular business structure.

Developing A Business Plan

While there are some entrepreneurs out there who have started businesses without a solid plan and have succeeded, they are an anomaly. What made them succeed was an entrepreneurial drive, great timing, solid business skills, and some luck. You can have all of these and still create a business plan to make your chances of success even greater. A business plan is especially useful if this will be your first business. While there is no guarantee that you will succeed with a plan, the odds will be in your favor.

Many startup business owners will dismiss a proper plan because they see it as a way to convince lenders and investors about the viability of the business. However, the goal of the plan should be to convince you about whether your ideas and objectives make sense and are obtainable. Besides, it is your money, time, and effort that are on the line. Why not set yourself up to succeed the best you can?

The basics of a business plan should include:

- A strategic process to start building.
- A strong marketing and sales plan.
- A foundation for the smooth operation of the business.
- Your current position and where you want to be. What gaps are there between the two?
- A plan for persuading a lender or investor to come on board with their proposal.

Many entrepreneurs learn from the moment they create their plan whether their design is good or not. From this point, they decide whether to move forward with their idea or not. Business owners who don't make a plan often learn the hard way that their business model was doomed to fail. Developing a business plan ahead of time can save you a lot of money and headache. Starting a business is not cheap. So, you want to make sure you understand what you're walking into.

At the minimum, your plan should be logical and objective. Try to take any emotion out of it. It is always possible to become so overwhelmed with excitement that you conveniently look past potential holes in your blueprint and future execution. If you can't look at your plan objectively, try reaching out to a trusted friend to get their input. After some good analysis, a once-promising business plan can prove not to be as viable as once thought, due to a variety of factors. Some of these factors include a saturated market for the product and service you're providing, insufficient funds, or perhaps even a nonexistent market. Basically, no one would ever buy your product because it has no mass appeal. It may not have been a bad idea; it is just bad timing because it is way ahead of its time.

If you tried to introduce some of the products, we have now 20 to 30 years ago, they probably would have flopped, mainly because there was no need for them. An example of this would have been a smartphone in the 1990s when people were still trying to figure the internet out.

The plan you make should also serve as a guide to business operations for the first month and even years down the line. Of course, many things can change, so long-term plans need to be flexible.

A solid business plan will clearly communicate the company's vision and purpose for existing. This will be the main reason for the business. It should also detail the responsibilities of management, personnel, and an evaluation of current and future competition. The competition does not even have to be direct. For example, if you have a coffee shop, and there is a donut shop down the street that starts selling coffee, that could hurt your business. Even if their coffee is not as good or provides the same variety, people may buy it from there out of pure convenience.

Finally, you can create a financial proposal for an investor or lender if you choose to go this route. They will evaluate your proposal and determine whether your business is a solid investment based on your plan. Overall, a good business plan should be convincing both to you and everyone else involved. If you are seeking capital, you must convince those you are seeking it from that your business has great potential. They are taking a financial risk too, so they must be excited about what you present them.

Furthermore, if you plan on having employees, then they must be convinced too that your business idea is well thought out and organized. This is especially true when you are new and not established yet. Potential employees will do their research because they want to ensure proper payment and that the business will be successful for the long haul. The last thing they want is to get a job and then have to look for another one a few weeks later.

Once again, the first person you need to convince is yourself. If you are not confident after creating your business plan, then you have two options: Scrap the whole idea, or take a step back and refine a few things. The decision is yours based on what the analysis tells you.

The Different Sections of a Business Plan

We will now get into several different sections of a business plan and how you can build one for yourself. A plan like this is not something you just put down on a piece of scratch paper. It needs to be an official document that is well written. It may be something you have to present to people at some point. These individuals will not appreciate trying to read a bunch of incoherent language. The following are the separate components of a startup plan from beginning to end. We will just provide a summary of what each part entails.

Executive Summary:

This section presents a brief outline of the company's purpose and objectives. An executive summary will include:

- A quick description of the products and/or services that will be provided.
- A list of the main objectives.
- A description of the current market that your company will be a part of.
- Justification of the viability of your idea, including what will make your company stand out from everyone else.
- A summary of the growth potential. How likely is it your company will continue to expand in the future?
- A summary of the requirements for funding the business.

This is the first section of the business plan and often what will determine if someone you are presenting it to will read any further. If the executive summary is poorly written, then the rest of this document will become meaningless in that sense. Your summary needs to identify what problem your business is ready to solve for the public. For example, if many pools need their tiles cleaned, then your summary needs to present that in an obvious way. Think of it as a snapshot or elevator pitch that you can regurgitate to someone quickly, and they will know exactly what you are talking about.

Overview and Objectives:

Providing an overview of your company can be tricky if you are just starting. To make it simple, consider the following guidelines:

- What products or services will you provide?
- How will you provide them?
- What do you need at your disposal to provide them? (Location, equipment, etc.)
- Who will provide the items? (Trained staff?)
- Whom will the items be provided for? Who are your target customers?

Once you have these questions answered, then you will have a better overview of your business. After this, then you can start focusing on some of the basics like:

- Identify and define what industry your business falls under. For example, food, retail, manufacturing, healthcare, or wholesale.

- Identify who your main customer base will be, and be as specific as you can: young adult women, teenagers, senior citizens over 60, or people with particular limitations. Until you know who your customers are, you cannot market to them. Do not put your customers as "everybody" unless it will serve everybody, like a restaurant or convenience store.

- Explain what problems you are solving for the customer. Any good business is solving some sort of problem for the public. Figure out what that is for you, and define it well. For example, a mini mart can solve a problem by providing a variety of items quickly and conveniently so people don't have to go to a major supermarket.

Products and Services:

In this section, you will describe the actual product or service you are providing. Make sure to use simple terms that the mass public can understand as there may be some technical terms or industry words that most of the population is not aware of. The goal is to be descriptive but understandable.

You must also use this section to detail how your product or service is different from your competition. Why should they do business with you rather than the person down the street from their house? Patents, copyrights, and trademarks that you own should also be listed in this section. The following are some key questions to answer:

- Do your products or services already exist, and are they ready to go, or are they still in the developmental stages? How soon will they be ready to market? Perhaps you're creating a new clothing line and waiting for the inventory.
- Are there significant advantages to what you're providing over your competition?
- What are your operating costs, and are they low enough to create a reasonable profit margin?
- How will you acquire your products or provide your services? Are there multiple manufacturers involved?

Market Opportunities:

Market research is essential to a business's success. Your business plan needs to analyze and evaluate the demographics of your intended customers, their purchasing habits and cycles, and their willingness to use new and unfamiliar products and services. If you don't have customers, you don't have a business. So, do as much research as you can. Consider some of the following questions regarding the market and the industry you are in:

- What is the size of your target market, and what is the potential for growth or decline in the future?
- What are the growth prospects of the industry as a whole? Is there expected growth or decline?
- What is the demand for the specific product or service you are selling? Is this demand expected to stay high?
- Can you separate yourself from the competition in a meaningful way for your customers?
- What will your customers be expecting to pay for the products or services? If you're charging more than the competition, why?

Sales and Marketing:

The bottom line here is that you can provide the greatest product or service in the world, but if nobody knows it exists, then it's meaningless. This is why a solid sales and marketing plan is imperative. Don't think of marketing as just advertisements; it is also investments to help your company grow and prosper. Once you decide to go into business, marketing will be a part of your life until the end.

With this investment mindset, you must also understand that the money you put into marketing must generate a return greater than the initial investment. If it's not, then your marketing is useless. Do your best research and create a smart and effective marketing plan. Here are some of the basic steps involved:

- Focus on your target customers and determine the best way to reach them.
- Evaluate your competition and determine how your marketing plan can set you apart. Standing out from the crowd is hard, especially if you don't know who the crowd is. This is why it's important to know your competition.
- Consider the brand that you are putting out. Does it give off attractive vibes? Your brand will determine how your customers will perceive you. Perception is reality and will also impact your sales.
- Once again, focus on the problems you are solving, and let the customers know about them. Customers don't care as much about the actual product or service as they do about the benefits, they will receive from it.

Consider what your budget is for sales and marketing. Find the cheapest options you can, but make sure they are effective. Of course, having an online presence through social media, a website, or both is critical. Never be shy about talking about your business. If you don't believe in it, no one else will either.

One thing to remember is that when your business becomes well known, people will start associating it with you a lot more. They may do that from the beginning. This means that whenever you are in the public eye, you are representing your business in some way.

Competitive Advantage:

This section is devoted to analyzing your competition, both current and potential. Every business has competition, so it is to your advantage to understand their strengths and weaknesses. You need to do a thorough assessment regularly because when you let your guard down, your customers will start to leave. This can be a complicated process, but here are some of the basics to consider:

- Profile your current competitors by looking at their websites, studying their marketing plans, and assessing their strengths and weaknesses.
- Identify potential competitors by looking at potential growth in the marketplace.
- Look at who your primary and secondary competitors are.
- Determine what opportunities you provide to your customers.

Operations:

Your operations plan is basically how you will run and operate your business daily. It should detail the strategies from the different sections of your business, like managing, staffing, manufacturing, and inventory. The operations section is often the easiest part of running a business. However, this does not mean it won't be tough, so a solid plan is still necessary. Consider the following questions when looking into your operation's needs:

- What supplies, equipment, and facilities will you need? Can the business be run from your home, or will you need to find another location?
- What will be the organizational structure? Who will be responsible for specific aspects of the company like accounting or stocking?
- What will your staffing needs be like, and will you need additional staff in the future?
- What business relationships will you need to acquire, and how do you plan on getting those? Will these relationships affect your day-to-day operations?
- How will processes change as your company grows?
- What cost-saving measures can you take part in?

Your operations plans will be specific to your company, industry, and customers. A few other items you need to consider are zoning requirements, building or renovation costs, the space needed, and accessibility for the customers.

Management Team:

The quality and experience of the management team will be a major factor for many investors and lenders. This is how they determine the potential for business success. Of course, having a strong management team will also be beneficial for your business. The following are some key questions to consider:

- Who are the key leaders, and what is their background as far as education, experience, and skill set?
- Do these key leaders have experience in your industry, and if not, what relevant experience do they bring to the table? For example, someone may not know your industry, but they may have great leadership skills.
- What duties will each person on the team be responsible for, and how much authority will they be given? Once this is established, it is important not to step on each other's feet. For example, if someone on the management team brings down disciplinary action on an employee, per his role, then he should not be challenged unless it is necessary.
- What will the salary structure be, and what levels will be required to attract employees for each position?

Financial Analysis:

To put it simply: money talks. The ultimate reason for a business is to make a profit. Financial projections are what will be evaluated by investors and lenders to determine a company's potential for success. This will be how you know if your business has a good chance of becoming viable. The following are some reports that will help evaluate financial estimates for the future:

- Balance sheet: This describes the company's cash position in assets, liabilities, shareholders, and earnings retained. It will show the financial health of the company.
- Income statement: This is also called a profit and loss statement, and it will show if a company will be profitable during a given period.
- Cash flow statement: A project of cash receipts and expense payments. This statement shows how and when cash will flow through the business.
- Operating budget: Provides a detailed breakdown of income and expenses.
- Break-even analysis: A projection of how much revenue is needed to cover fixed and variable expenses. This is the minimum income that a business needs to break even.

Remember that this is just an overview of a business plan. It is certainly a lot and intimidating at first, but do not skip this step. Even if you don't intend to show the plan to anyone else, at least do it for yourself. Don't think of this task as a necessary evil. Instead, see it as a major steppingstone to building your business. If you think developing a business plan is stressful, imagine the anxiety that comes from a failed business because of a lack of preparation.

The great thing about a detailed business plan is that most of the potential problems can be discovered during this process. Deciding to open a business can be exciting when you first come up with the idea. If you feel the same way after writing out your business plan, that is a good sign. But once again, take emotion out of it and look at your report objectively and logically.

If you found this book to be valuable, then please help other people learn about it by leaving a review.

Chapter 5

Investing

When we think about business and the entrepreneurial spirit, we think about the person who took his entire life's savings and put it into a product he believed in. We think about the person who opened a restaurant and wanted it to succeed so badly that he slept at night on a cot in one of the back rooms. We think about the person who leaves before the sun rises, works nonstop during the day, and does not come home until well after the sun goes down. These people do not work the 9-5 business hours. They work until the tasks are done, and then they start over the next day. They don't rely on a salary or hourly wage. They rely on their businesses bringing in the income they need. These are the individuals we think of when we think about people who run their businesses.

Running a business is a lot of hard work and sacrifice. One of the biggest determinants of the success of a business is the investment that the business owner is willing to put in. This is not exclusive to money; the time and effort required are also important. There is no sugarcoating it. There is a lot of uncertainty in owning a business, and there will be days where you feel like quitting. The rewards from running a successful business, though, are tremendous. This chapter will focus on the importance of investing in your business initially and throughout the years that you operate it. We will discuss the importance of putting your profits back into your business and using them for other investments that will bring in more profits.

We will also detail the importance of using your time appropriately since you will be investing a lot of it into your business. Since your business is an extension of you, investing in it also means you are investing in yourself.

How to Get Initial Capital

When you are first starting your business, you will have to make a major investment in the form of initial capital. This will be used to start the business, including buying the necessary items like inventory, equipment, a building or physical location, licenses, and various other expenses. All of this depends on the type of business you are starting. Unless you are lucky enough to have a trust fund, you will need to find ways to get initial capital. In 2016, around 73% of businesses used some form of financing (Wood, 2017). If you are in this camp, then consider some of the following ways to raise capital for your business.

Bootstrapping Your Business:

This means that you are paying all of your business expenses yourself without taking out a loan. This can be done as long as the business does not require a large initial capital. If you don't have enough in savings, then you can apply for a 0% interest business credit card that will allow you to borrow cash for a short period without any recurring interest. If you invest your own money initially, investors will be more willing to partner with you down the line.

Ask Friends or Family:

Seek out friends or family who you trust and who also have business experience. They should also understand risk as they are initially investing in your company. Before you ask, you must have a sound plan set up and communicate it well. Make sure to keep track of the loan and payments being made back to it.

Angel Investors:

Angel investors are accredited individuals with a net worth of more than $1 million or an annual income of more than $200,000. You may work with an individual investor or a team. Angel investors can be a great source of capital, but you must have your business plan set up and be ready to give an enticing pitch. They must see that you are passionate about your business; otherwise, they won't be either.

Apply for a Business Loan:

This is the most typical way that new business owners find capital. Small business loans are probably going to give you the most favorable rates. You can apply for these at your financial institution.

Investing in Your Business

People tend to spend what they earn. When someone receives a paycheck from work, they immediately spend it on goodies that they want. This also occurs with business owners. Instead of managing their profits intelligently, they end up spending everything on useless items. None is left to reinvest back into their business. This is unfortunate because if you want your business to succeed in the long run, you must be willing to invest in it.

After the initial investment is made, many business owners believe they are done in this area. This could not be further from the truth. The initial investment is just the starting point. Use your income stream the correct way, and start putting it back into your business.

The Benefits of Investing in Your Business

Investing in your business is not just a talking point. There are numerous advantages that it will create for you. While it can be tempting to take your revenue and spend it on things you enjoy, your business will ultimately suffer, and the profits you enjoy will stop coming in until your business shuts down completely. The following are some of the benefits of investing back into your business.

Your Business Will Grow:

For your business to grow, you have to make it grow. No matter how cliché it may sound, you need to spend money to earn money. Spending on your business will help you earn more money in the future. When you think about your business, think in terms of long-term growth rather than short-term profits. Unfortunately, people become blinded by the money that is pouring in, and they believe it will last forever. As a result, they begin ignoring small aspects of their business and forget that an income stream can stop at any time. If they have not invested in the growth of their business, they will be left in the dust.

The investments you make can be in things like newer products that provide extra convenience, outsourcing certain tasks so that you have more time to focus on other aspects of the business, and staying up to date on technology and marketing services. As your business grows, you have to grow with it. You have to give up some of the responsibilities by delegating. You must also be willing to change with the times. The recent pandemic showed us that businesses need to be flexible and continue updating themselves. Unfortunately, many of the businesses that went under during this tumultuous time were stuck in the past and refused to move forward.

You Will Take Your Business More Seriously:

Once you invest more in your business, you will take it more seriously because you have more on the line. This is because you want to make sure your investment is worth it. You will not want to waste the money that you have earned.

Other people will take your business more seriously too. This includes your customers. When they see you willing to invest in your business, they will recognize that you are in it for the long haul. They will more likely want to do business with you, whether they are customers or vendors.

You Will Feel Less Stressed:

This relates to using your revenue to invest in outside help. This will allow many of the tasks that are either menial or out of your scope to be handled by someone else. This will be a huge timesaver, which will allow you to focus on the more important aspects of your business that require your attention. Many of the small tasks often take twice as long when we do them ourselves. This is because we are not as familiar with them. Once you hire an expert, not only will it save you time, but it will also be done right. Just make sure you bring on a dependable person. When you start investing in people and their services to make your life go smoother, you will have much less stress.

You Can Focus on What You're Best At:

This goes along the lines of the previous benefit. Once you are not bogged down with unfamiliar tasks, you will have more time to focus on what you excel at. Do what you do best and then hire the rest. Most successful businesspeople are successful because they surrounded themselves with the right people. They did not dare do everything themselves.

You Will Save Time:

When you invest in people and updated technology, you will save a lot of time, which will open up your schedule for things that truly require your attention.

There are numerous other reasons why investing in your business is beneficial. We could write a separate book just discussing those benefits. The above five will give you a good idea of why investing is important, though. You will not regret investing in your business. The only investment you will feel bad about is the one you didn't make.

How to Invest in Your Business

Now that we know about the benefits of investing in your own business, we will go over some of the best ways to invest your company's profits. Remember that if it is helping your business in some way, then the money is not being wasted. So, how should you invest that dollar or two that you've earned?

Business Improvement:

This one is pretty obvious. A part of your revenue should go back to create improvements within your business and its structure. Investing in business improvements can include things like infrastructure, equipment, upgraded technology, or streamlining business processes. It does not have to be something that is broken. It can also mean upgrading in certain areas.

Instead of focusing on the percentage that you will reinvest back, pay attention to your plan for improvement. For example, if you are planning some major revisions within your company, you may need a little more capital to pull them off. Investing in improvements like this can mean increased profits in the future because of higher productivity and happier customers.

Marketing:

Marketing your business will be a never-ending campaign. You always need to keep your business's name out there so future customers will know about it. Digital marketing, when done properly, is a smart investment that will increase profits.

Invest in Your Team:

Invest in your team to build a better workforce. This will increase productivity and streamline your business. You will also be able to create an attractive work environment, which employees seek when looking for jobs. You can reinvest your profits into things like extra training and continuing education. You can also begin offering higher benefits packages and various incentive programs. When you invest in your team, your staff will be happier, which means there will be less turnover.

Hire Extra Help:

At first, you may need to wear several hats as a business owner. With increased profits, you can use that money to invest in more help. For example, bring someone in to do your bookkeeping and free yourself up for other tasks.

Get Help from a Coach:

If you are having a hard time coming up with a strategic plan, consider hiring a career coach to help you. These experts are well versed in executive leadership, business strategies, working with investors, and handling various workplace conflicts. The education you receive will be worth it.

Improve Your SEO:

SEO stands for search engine optimization, which is a technique used to get your website and other online pages to the top of search engine results. This can be tricky, but you'll get the hang of it over time. If not, you can also hire an expert to do it for you. If you don't have a website, then create one ASAP.

Create a Cash Buffer:

While reinvesting your profits back into your business, also set aside some money as a cash buffer. This will be used as your emergency fund in case problems arise. Having some liquid cash is always handy.

These are some of the top ways to reinvest your money back into your business. If you can come up with other ways to help your business grow, consider them too.

Investing Outside of Your Business

While we recommend that you reinvest your early profits solely into your business, once you start bringing in more revenue, you can start diversifying your portfolio. If you can use the profits from your business to create more money somewhere else, then you can eventually form multiple streams of income, which will be great for you and your business.

Putting your money from your business into solid investments can help your money grow year after year. This will continue to grow your wealth exponentially. A diversified portfolio will be better for your financial future. Just remember to keep reinvesting in your business too because that will help ensure continued growth in that aspect. In addition, you can put the income you make from outside investments back into your business. It becomes a cycle of profitable investments.

The following are some of the top investments you can place your money into.

Real Estate:

Real estate has always been a solid investment that has made people a lot of money. If you hold on to a piece of property long enough, it almost always goes up in value. Buying commercial real estate and then renting it out to another business is a great way to bring in some steady cash flow each month. In addition, you can buy a home and rent it out to a family or individual. You can benefit from the monthly revenue while you are waiting for it to go up in value.

Make sure you do your research and do not just buy the first property that you see. You want to make sure it has the potential for growth financially. Also, if you are financing the property, make sure the mortgage and other expenses will be covered by the rent payments.

Stocks and Mutual Funds:

You don't have to invest in individual stocks here. That takes time and skill. What you can do is open up various investment accounts through a bank, investment firm, or other financial institution. Some good examples of these accounts are mutual funds, index funds, and IRAs. Each type of account comes with its risks and benefits. It is best to speak with a financial advisor to get the best information.

High-interest savings accounts or a certificate of deposit are also good accounts to keep your money in. They ensure continued income and are FDIC insured, unlike the investment accounts we mentioned previously.

The bottom line is that as you bring in more income through your business, make sure that money is not wasted. Use it wisely to increase your wealth even further. Investing in your business is an investment in yourself.

Chapter 6

Starting an Online Business

Imagine owning a multi-million-dollar business that brings in great annual revenue and allows you to live the life of your dreams. Now, imagine that you can run this business without leaving your home. In fact, you can run it while you're at the park, in your favorite coffee shop, or on vacation. It may sound too good to be true, but it is possible with an online business.

We are not saying that you will become a millionaire, but the potential for great revenue is there. You can start an online business and replace the income from a job or even exceed it. The great thing about online businesses is that they usually require much less initial capital and investment than a business requiring a physical location. You will have much more flexibility in running the business since you can hop on the computer and get to work. Of course, there is always the benefit of never having to leave your home.

If you fear starting a brick-and-mortar business, especially in light of a pandemic, then consider going the online business route. It may be what you have been looking for this whole time.

Online Business Options

There are numerous online business ideas out there, and many of them do not require anything more than an internet connection. You will have the freedom to work from almost anywhere that has a strong signal. Also, while it is nearly impossible to run more than one business that requires a physical location, it is much more practical to have multiple online businesses at the same time. If you find more than one of the businesses mentioned in this section interesting, then consider trying out all of those options. Just don't overwhelm yourself too much. Even online businesses have their challenges.

Drop shipping:

Drop shipping is a great option if you want to start an e-commerce site. The great thing with this option is that you are not required to carry any inventory. You can just take customer orders on your online store and have them sent directly to a third-party retailer. At this point, you just need to make sure you sell the item for a higher price than you buy it, and you will earn a nice profit.

Online Tutor:

If you have a good internet connection, are knowledgeable in a particular subject, and are great at explaining things, then becoming an online tutor may be right up your alley. You can use a video chatting system like Skype to conduct video calls and do tutoring sessions remotely. You get to help someone learn a new subject and make some extra money.

Résumé and Cover Letter Writer:

If you have skill and knowledge in creating masterful résumés and cover letters, then you can offer these services through many online platforms like social media or freelance sites like Upwork, Fiverr, and Thumbtack. LinkedIn is a great site too for creating business contacts. Write a résumé or cover letter for anyone willing to hire you. Be mindful that certain sites, like Upwork, have higher-than-normal fees.

Social Media Consultant:

Large corporations often hire various agencies to run their social media accounts for them, but small businesses often handle their own. This is mainly because they don't have the capital to hire an agency. These business owners are often so overwhelmed with everything else that upkeep on their social media accounts is almost impossible. As a social media consultant, you can help these small business owners by determining the best tactics, posting schedules, and content for their target audience. Once their followers begin to grow, so will your business.

Most of your work will probably be on Facebook and Twitter since these are still the largest social media platforms. However, other sites like Tumblr, Instagram, and Snapchat are popular too. If you have some social media marketing experience, then this is a great option for earning cash flow.

SEO Consultant:

If you have a deep knowledge of search engines and technical skills in platforms like Google Ads, then becoming an SEO consultant is a great option for you. You can start educating small business owners about the benefits of SEO and the impact it can have on their business. You can help transform their website so they have a much stronger online presence and higher conversion rates. Remember that Google's algorithms are always changing, so you need to keep up with your SEO education.

Blogger:

If you have a passion for writing and have a lot of great information to share, then blogging may be the right option for you. As a blogger, you can write about almost any topic, and if there is an audience for it, you can bring in some great revenue. Websites like Weebly and WordPress make starting a blog simple. The key to success here is consistency and quality. This means that you have to write often, and your articles have to be well written. While they do not have to be college essays, they cannot be riddled with spelling, grammar, and punctuation errors. It will just make you look unprofessional and sloppy. Your content also has to be informative, educational, and entertaining so people will continue to follow you.

Once you hone your skills and build an audience, you can start selling ad space or sponsor posts on your site. Also, once you become an authority in your subject matter, you can begin selling online courses, e-books, and webinars. The opportunities are abundant here.

Virtual Assistant:

If you have impeccable organizational skills, pay attention to detail, and can manage multiple tasks well at the same time, then you should look into becoming a virtual assistant. The services mainly consist of basic administrative tasks, making travel arrangements, responding to emails, and making phone calls. If you have previous administrative experience, that is great, but it is not necessary. TaskRabbit and Virtual are good sites to find jobs like these.

Affiliate Marketer:

Affiliate marketers leave reviews for various products on sites like Amazon. This is a great source of marketing for many companies, and they are willing to share a portion of their profits with persuasive individuals like yourself. So, if you want to get paid for leaving positive reviews for products you already use, consider becoming an affiliate marketer.

These are just a few of the online business opportunities that are available to you. There are many more out there that you can get into based on your interests. The internet has opened the door to so many money-making options, and if you do enough research, you are bound to find something that piques your interest. You will see that the opportunities are endless.

With any online business, the main thing you will need is a good computer and internet connection. If you take your business on the road, try to find locations with good Wi-Fi. You can also invest in a mobile hotspot device, which will allow you to carry your Wi-Fi as you travel. Depending on the particular business, you may also need specific software. These are all essential investments to make when going digital.

The Challenges of Online Business

While online business provides numerous benefits and might be the best option for long-term success, you should still be aware of the disadvantages or issues that can arise. You will be met with your own set of challenges, and the more you are aware of them, the better prepared you will be.

Cybersecurity:

Online security is a major issue, and if you are not careful, a lot of important and highly personal information can be extracted from you and placed into the wrong hands. There are highly sophisticated crimes that can be done online within seconds, and you need a sophisticated framework to protect yourself, your employees, and your customers. Also, since online businesses cannot shut down operations without losing a lot of revenue, their online space is vulnerable to an attack.

Large online platforms usually have something in place, but small businesses often ignore this fact. All businesses that operate online need a cybersecurity framework in place and policies to combat these attacks. There must be a thorough incident response plan in case of a breach. All these interventions can reduce the need for downtime in operations, plus they give you more online security. The last thing you want with a successful online business is for all of your hard work to go down the drain due to a cyberattack.

Order Fulfillment:

With an online business, you will generally have more access to customers due to the far-reaching capabilities of the internet. Your customers may even exist all over the world if your strategy is good enough. This is positive, but the challenge will come when you need to fill your orders. This can take up a lot of your time and effort, especially considering the packing and shipping. If you can hire a third-party to take care of the order-fulfillment tasks, it will save you a lot of precious time so you can focus on other aspects of your business.

Competition:

Online business has taken off tremendously over the past few years. This means that you will be competing for pricing with people from around the world. Your prices need to be competitive, and your product needs to stand out in some way.

Customer Experience:

The advantage of having a typical brick-and-mortar business is that it's easier to create a positive customer experience due to face-to-face communication. This can be much more difficult to achieve with an online business. Generally, customers are just looking at a web page of some sort, and no matter how nice it is, physical presence is much more effective. Nonetheless, it is not impossible to achieve a positive customer experience.

There are ways to make your website more welcoming. You can also post regular video chats with customers and have friendly pictures and promotional videos of yourself. In addition, competitive pricing and prompt service will always be appreciated. Remember that whether it is online or offline, your customers expect to be treated well.

Visibility:

Since you will not have a fancy storefront or physical location, you will have to rely on people finding you on the internet among millions of other websites. This can make or break your online business. This is where SEO really comes into play. Your company must have some keywords that will bring it to the top of a Google search. The goal is for people to find you, even if they don't know your name. If you do not understand SEO, then take the time to learn it, or hire someone who can help you.

Having an online business will bring in a lot of potential for great income. In light of the ever-changing world we live in, where many things are going digital, it makes more sense to go this route than to create a business that requires a physical location. While many traditional businesses have had to shut down, the online sector has thrived. You can create your own online business and do well; just consider the challenges and setbacks you may face.

The Biggest Mistakes That People Make

Many of the challenges of online business are also due to mistakes that people make. In business, mistakes are inevitable and often unforeseeable. These blunders may not ruin your business; they might just create some setbacks. Other, more prominent errors could bring down your whole company. The more familiar you are with common mistakes, the less likely you are to make them. Entrepreneurship is tough enough, so why not figure out ways to make your life simpler?

Waiting Too Long to Launch:

While you want as many of your ducks in a row as possible, delaying the launch of a business can be detrimental to its success. There will never be a perfect time to start. Conditions will never be perfect. However, this cannot stop you from pushing forward. Whether it's finances, time constraints, or being afraid, sometimes, you need to just have some faith and make the jump. Waiting too long can make you and the public disinterested. The longer you wait, the more you will think and overthink, and the more likely you will talk yourself out of it.

If you have a great idea, chances are that other people will too. If these other people don't let their mindset stop them, then they will have an early advantage and might even take over the market. As a result, you will be left in limbo.

Also, industries and public opinions change. What garnered a lot of public interest before can become old news down the line. Think about how much things have changed just in the past few years. Not striking while the iron is hot can mean that you miss out on major income opportunities. It is nearly impossible to predict what will catch on with the public, but once you've done your research and prepared as much as you can, it's time to trust your gut and take the leap.

Going at It Alone:

People believe that because it is their business or their idea, they must go at it alone. Honestly, you should not go at it alone. We spoke earlier about the importance of delegation. If some tasks or factors require advanced training, like accounting, then it is best to have some extra hands on deck. People hesitate to pay someone, mainly because of low funding abilities. However, if you can hire someone to take a few things off your plate, then your mind can be open and free to handle other areas of the business. In the long run, you will have more success and financial gain. When you are running a business, consider your time as more valuable than money. When you spend money for extra help, think of it as an investment that will create a return.

Not Being Different:

There is a great reference out there related to the game of Tetris. You may have played or heard of this game before. The concept is that you need to take blocks of various shapes and sizes and fit them into specific spaces. As you create some congruence, the blocks disappear, which is the objective of the game. Becoming good at this game requires skill and effort. The problem is that it also teaches us that the way to garner success is to fit.

We are here to turn this myth on its side. When it comes to business, the last thing you want is to fit in because you will not be different than anyone else. It will be even harder to stand out and create success. To gain attention, you must be different in some way. You must not try to simply fit in or you and your business will disappear figuratively and, eventually, literally.

Standing apart from your competition is essential, especially since there will be products and services like yours. Going online makes this problem much worse because it is harder to stand out behind a computer screen. Your uniqueness may not always showcase itself online. You must put in extra effort to make this happen. Never be afraid of being different.

Solving a Problem That Is Not Relevant:

We have spoken throughout this book about the importance of solving a problem with a business idea. This idea must be relevant so enough people will care about it. If you are solving a problem of little importance to the general public, then your idea will not get any steam. Do your research on society and determine what issues people have. After this determination, figure out how to solve the problem in question. This does not have to be complicated. For example, when cell phones came out, people were terrified of dropping and breaking them. As a result, someone came up with the idea of phone cases.

This goes along the lines of listening to customers before and while you are running a business. Your customers must feel like you're talking to them directly. If you are coming up with solutions to their problems, they will not just see you as a businessperson. They will see you as a close companion who cares about their needs. If you've heard about a problem on the internet, there is probably more than one person thinking about it.

Having Unrealistic Expectations:

Here is something you need to understand: If you are getting into business because you want some get-rich-quick scheme, you need to change your mindset. It can take businesses years to start turning a profit. This time may be reduced with online businesses. Nonetheless, if you plan to start making money right away, step back and understand what you are getting yourself into.

Your business will take time to gain momentum, so please put away any grandiose ideas of instant wealth. Expect to put in some time and effort into your idea. Also, don't be hard on yourself if it's taking longer than expected. Having unrealistic expectations will be detrimental to your psyche and cause you to become disinterested. Always keep your end goal in mind, and keep working toward it.

Setting Goals:

Speaking of goals, you must have them to create a business, or you will be completely lost. This would be like driving on the road with no end destination. You will never get where you need to be. Also, remember that goals do not have to be a final destination. You can have several attainable goals and make more along the way as you achieve them.

Online Businesses and the Pandemic

According to the *Wall Street Journal*, the Covid-19 pandemic is deepening the national divide between traditional and online businesses (Tory, 2020). It is easy to see why. Since there so many new restrictions were put in place, some businesses were forced to close their doors due to being deemed nonessential and people not willing to go out, either out of fear or inconvenience. Several analysts are saying this divide will continue to grow quickly after the pandemic. As a society, we were already headed in this direction anyway; the pandemic just accelerated things.

While some brick-and-mortar businesses have shuttered their doors, online merchants have seen growth like never before. How large and wide will this divide go? It is difficult to predict. It's hard to imagine a world where everything will be online, but we shall see what the future holds. Just realize that if your dream is to still run a business, the online option is the way to do it for better chances of success. Also, as we mentioned before, your business must have an online presence no matter what type it is.

Consider some of the following examples as further indication of the online shift:

- Doctors, therapists, and other health-care professionals are offering telemedicine services where they sit in their office while communicating with their patients digitally. They can even prescribe medications through a video call and email a prescription. Of course, medicine still requires a physical presence to a degree. We do not have online hospitals or procedures just yet.

- New online counseling options are popping up regularly.
- Yoga and other fitness classes are now offered online through Zoom and other online video options.
- Schools and universities have moved their classes online. This is one that was forced due to the pandemic.

These instances showcase how nontraditional online industries are veering in that direction too. This can be scary for those who are old-school and stuck in their ways, but it is exciting for others who are ready to grow, change, and prosper. Of course, if you get into business and don't have the mindset for the latter, then you are coming in with the wrong thought process anyway. A few decades ago, you may not have had to worry about constant changes, but in our new, fast-paced, and ever-changing world, you cannot afford not to worry about this.

Online business is truly a new revolution that is happening, and we do not see it slowing down anytime soon. Check out some of the futuristic shows like *Star Trek* or *The Jetsons*. These shows were fictional, but they still reveal a lot about the future world. In fact, we are already seeing some of the technologies from those shows in our present world.

Just research various types of online business options. You will not believe what is out there, and the ones we mentioned in this chapter are just the tip of the iceberg. You may get clever and come up with something original. Just remember, consider existing problems, and figure out a way to solve them.

Another thing to note is that online businesses did not go unscathed during the pandemic. One of the biggest issues was the increased time for shipping and handling. Operations at every level were affected to a certain degree, so online businesses took some of the brunt as well.

It is important to listen to your customers. They are not saying what they say to be mean. At least, most of them aren't. Their feedback, whether positive or negative, will provide you with a lot of valuable information. Take in all of it and decipher the constructive from the nonconstructive.

Chapter 7

Social Media for Business

What did you do when you woke up today? If you are like many people, you may have gotten on social media. You quickly got caught up on everything that happened since the last time you checked, which was probably the night before. All of a sudden, it's been 30 minutes or an hour, and all you have done is scroll through social media. The biggest problem with this is that it was a total time waster, assuming that you were not doing any type of business on one of these platforms.

Social media has created a unique and effective way for people to keep in touch with each other, even if they live on opposite sides of the globe. Friends and family have been able to reconnect. Lines of communication have opened, and people have much more access to the entire world. All of this is great. The problem is that people get caught up in drama, long and useless conversations, or mindless scrolling. This is neither productive nor healthy.

Wouldn't it be great if social media could be used for business purposes? Well, your wish is our command because that is exactly what we will be discussing in this chapter. Social media, regardless of the platform, can be used to make money through various channels, or it can be a major marketing tool for another business. Stop the endless time-wasting that comes with Facebook, Instagram, Twitter, or any other social media site. Start using them to your advantage and create revenue like you never could before.

Advertising on the Various Platforms

Those of you reading this book might be more familiar with the various types of social media platforms out there. There seem to be new ones popping up every day. For this section, we will be focusing on some of the biggest ones that the vast majority of the population uses.

We have discussed the importance of marketing your business throughout this book. It is one of the constants no matter what type of business you have. It is hard to remember a time when social media was not a part of our lives. In reality, it hasn't been that long in relation to history. If you were born in the early 1990s or before, then you had some formidable years without any social media. Now, it is here and likely to stay forever. Many have capitalized on the power of social media to market their business, and it's time to jump on the bandwagon.

Through social media, you can connect with your audience in a powerful way to build your brand and increase your sales. You can also develop a deep connection with someone, even if you don't see them in person. At the start, social media started as a place to publish content to generate traffic to another website or actual business. However, it has matured over the past few years, and businesses use these sites in a myriad of ways.

For example, social media can be used for listening and engagement. This means that a business can monitor conversations on social media sites to determine what customers are saying about them. This is a great way to determine what is working and what is not. Several analytic tools can also be used to determine reach, engagement, and direct sales. Before you start publishing your content, consider some of the following ideas:

- What are your business goals and how can social media help you reach them? Do you need more brand awareness or sales, or do you need to drive traffic to websites? It may be all three and more.
- Which social media platforms do you want to focus on? Each one has advantages and setbacks, which we will discuss.
- What type of content do you want to share? This could be videos, images, links, or descriptions.

Remember that once people begin associating your social media account with your business, everything you post will be a reflection of it.

Planning and Publishing

To have any type of success on social media, you must have a regular presence. By that, we mean daily or several times a day. There are billions of people throughout the various platforms, so you need to make yourself visible by posting regularly. Make sure the content is relevant to your business, and don't just post a lot of filler. With a personal account, you do not have to be as mindful about the posting because it is simply read by friends, family, and a few followers. For a business social media account, you need to be aware of what you're posting so it is engaging. Be sure to keep your personal and business accounts separate.

Make sure you don't post everything at the same time. Time is limited and having to get on social media constantly to post is not always practical. Additionally, it can be hard to come up with interesting posts throughout the day. Try setting a specific time of day to write your posts. You can then schedule the posts to be released at scheduled times throughout the day by using various scheduling tools.

Different Platforms

We will now go over the different online platforms and how they can be used for marketing. Consider the advantages and disadvantages of each, and determine which ones are best to use for your business.

You may just use one or a combination of many for your marketing needs.

Facebook:

Despite some controversy over the past few years, Facebook is still the largest and most widely used platform for social media. If you can figure out a great way to market your business through this site, then you will have an extraordinary amount of reach. There are roughly 2.6 billion active users on a monthly basis on Facebook (Clement, 2020). If you learn to market your business and yourself properly, then the potential for your business to grow is limitless, especially if you have the ability to send products all over the world.

Facebook ads allow you to reach people based on age, gender, interests, lifestyles, life events, and several other factors. You can make the marketing extremely tailored toward your target audience. If you place an advertisement on Facebook, you will also have the option to put your ad across other areas, including Instagram and Messenger. The following are some of the advantages to Facebook marketing that you should consider:

- It is still the largest social media platform by far, so you will have a wide customer reach.
- The Ads Manager option allows you to remarket to users who have visited your website. You must install the Facebook Pixel code to your site.

- The Ads Manager also allows you to split test your ads on various audiences based on the factors mentioned earlier. This provides data for what works best and also helps to narrow your desired demographic.

- Lead generation ads allow potential customers to submit information about themselves to you. Customers can also request information about products or services that you provide. They can even schedule appointments through an ad form that appears on your feed. Customers never have to leave Facebook to fill out this form, which is a huge advantage.

- You can track or measure your conversions through Pixel. This allows you to see what actions users take after viewing your ads.

- Facebook marketing is cost-effective. You can run your ads for as little as a dollar per day and go up from there as needed.

- Facebook allows for full visibility so you can see how well your ads are doing based on what you spend. This is a great way to know if the ads are effective and if changes need to be made.

Facebook marketing has many advantages, and it is difficult to have a social media presence without a Facebook page. There are still some disadvantages to this pathway for you to be aware of, including:

- If you try to place an image with more than 20% of it covered in text, there's a high chance Facebook will reject it. This can be a case-by-case basis, but as a general guideline, the 20% rule is in effect.

- While Facebook's split testing is effective, it does not work as well as manual optimization.
- Facebook is huge. This means a lot of people advertise their businesses there. This vastly diminishes your ad's ability to stand out. You have to become creative, which may require additional costs. The marketing still won't break the bank, though.

The advantages outweigh the disadvantages. Try out Facebook if you have not already and see for yourself. Your business may get the boost that it needs.

Instagram:

Instagram has become extremely popular since its inception and is now a popular hub for businesses to market their products and services on. Business owners regularly post images of what they do to give their audience more of a visual representation. For example, barbers and hairstylists regularly post the haircuts they give to their clients so potential customers can see how good they are.

Instagram influencers also post regularly on this site. If an influencer is wearing a specific piece of clothing or eating at a particular restaurant, then it becomes major news immediately. That product or service garners a lot of attention. The following are some of the advantages of Instagram marketing:

- Instagram has over 100 million users, which pales in comparison to Facebook, but it is still a pretty significant number.
- About 90% of users are under the age of 35 and influenced heavily by what they see online.
- About 60% of users log in daily.
- Posts with texts may or may not catch someone's attention. Creating something visual, like a picture or video, will create much higher engagement. Imagery is a powerful marketing tool.

The following are some of the disadvantages of Instagram marketing:

- While the engagement on Instagram is high, the conversion rate is low. This means people are sharing, liking, and commenting on photos regularly, but their actions are not turning into dollars and cents.
- It can be difficult to stand out among all of the celebrities posting their content. How can you gain attention with your workout video when Terry Crews is posting on similar topics? You need to dedicate a lot of time to curating content that will resonate with the public.

It depends on what you're trying to market to determine whether Instagram will be a beneficial marketing tool. It is at least worth your time to do the research. If your product or service requires a lot of visuals, chances are this avenue will be worth it. For example, an accountant may not have as much engagement advantage on Instagram as a photographer, chef, artist, or fitness expert.

YouTube:

Yes, the video-hosting site that you watch all of your crazy videos on is also a social media platform you can use to market your business. With all of the insane content on here, you have to be smart about how to use it. Try to be as unique and creative as you can be. Practice your videos ahead of time and come up with ways, like background, lighting, and your behavior, that can be used to make you stand out. You must also upload regular content and make your videos look professional. The following are some of the advantages of YouTube marketing:

- YouTube is free to use. As long as you have a Google Gmail account, you can create a YouTube account too. You can also engage with others on the platform by liking or commenting on their videos.
- You can measure the analytics to determine how many views a particular video gets, plus where the viewers are from. As a

result, you can determine which region or groups of people enjoy your content the most.

- YouTube has a huge audience. Also, while many people are using this site to upload personal videos, few companies have dipped their foot into this channel as of now. It may be a great time to get onto this platform due to the reduced competition. Just make sure your videos are compelling.

The following are some of the disadvantages of YouTube:

- YouTube still has an unprofessional reputation, so viewers may not take you seriously, even if your videos are professional. This viewpoint is changing slowly.
- Videos can attract many negative and disgusting comments. It may not be something you did, but people seem to find a way to fight online no matter what. Suddenly, your comments section becomes filled with negative talk, which can make your video look bad. This is especially true if your video goes viral.

If you enjoy being in front of a camera and love talking, then YouTube is a great marketing option for you. Before uploading videos, look into the various programs, software, and equipment you can take advantage of to make your videos look stellar.

There are numerous social media sites beyond the ones mentioned above that can be used for marketing purposes. These include

Twitter, LinkedIn, Snapchat, and Tumblr, which are all popular and growing by the day. Use the ones that will give you the most advantages based on your particular company or industry. Some people like to use all of the platforms, and while this might work, if a particular site is not generating you any business, then it's just a waste of time and money. Also, there is such a thing as spreading yourself too thin on social media. This is when your business is splayed across multiple platforms, but not all of the platforms are valuable for your needs. Even though social media marketing is relatively inexpensive, you must still control your marketing budget.

Doing Direct Business on Social Media

Yes, social media is a great way to market your business. In addition, you can use various platforms to do business directly. You can build stores on these sites that allow you to sell products and services. If your page has a large and engaging audience, you can even receive revenue through other companies that want to market their businesses on your page. The opportunities to make money on social media continue to grow. The following are some examples of social media business opportunities.

Facebook Store:

Since Facebook is the largest social media platform out there, you can use it to create a store and sell products directly from the site. You'll just need to set up a Facebook business page and then learn their particular rules and regulations for shipping and receiving products. You can only sell physical products on Facebook, not digital services. Of course, you can still advertise these services and lead people to a site where they can buy them. Beyond this, you would set up your business just like anything else.

After starting a business page, you will then need to set up the store the way you want. This includes particular products you sell, the details of the business, and your contact information. Follow the various steps to fully set up your social media business. Facebook can be an efficient way to run an online store.

Instagram Store:

Instagram is another popular platform and a great place to create an online store. It has greater engagement than Facebook due to the imagery, but it still has less conversion. Facebook also owns Instagram, so to set up an Instagram shop, you must have a Facebook shop set up too. You can then link your Instagram account and follow the steps to set up your store. With the product pages on your Instagram shop, your customers can:

- See a product title and description
- View a product picture
- See the price
- Have a direct link to buy the product
- View similar products that you sell

Pinterest Store:

Pinterest is another site with millions of active users that can be used to sell your products. This site works as a digital pinboard that encourages you to curate and post all types of digital content. Pinterest users expect to see content that looks good and inspires them, whether they are images, GIFs, infographics, or videos. The following are a few ways you can sell your products through Pinterest:

- Promoted Pins: These pins are used as advertisements that business accounts pay for to guarantee reach toward a certain audience. Your audience can still interact with these pins, just like a standard pin.
- Rich Pins: These are highly optimized standard pins that offer a better experience for the users. Product rich pins can make shopping easier for Pinterest users by providing pricing, availability, and purchasing information. The other types of rich pins include apps, articles, and recipes, which all provide different features.
- Shop the Look Pins: These pins are exclusive to the fashion and home decor industries on Pinterest. Shoppers can easily find items and purchase them through the pin.

Become a Social Media Influencer:

Once you become an influencer on social media, you will have an effect on what other people buy and become interested in. When you gain a large and engaging audience, companies may start reaching out to you to market their products in some way. This is similar to a celebrity wearing a certain dress on the red carpet, which leads to people wanting the same dress. You do not have to be a celebrity, though, to become an influencer. Consider the following steps to create a bigger and more engaging audience:

1. Focus on a niche that you are interested in and can create content about. The narrower the niche, the better.

2. Choose your desired social media platforms to use. Just like with any other business, pick the one that gives you the most advantage. For example, a traveling niche may do well on Instagram because of the visuals involved.

3. Open a business account on the platform you're using.

4. Write an engaging bio. Write your story in a way that will garner attention.

5. Add a profile pic and cover photo that shows off the image you want to portray for your brand. Make sure the pic is of great quality and that your face is clearly visible. Consider your surroundings when taking a picture.

6. Understand your audience and who you are targeting. You cannot cater to everyone, and you must keep your loyal fan base.

7. Post relevant content for your followers. For example, if you are in the travel niche, then posting about finding cheap hotels that are still high quality will be beneficial.

8. Post consistently and regularly. Being absent for long periods creates disinterest.

9. Do not ignore the comments section. Engage with your audience as this shows that you care.

10. Show other brands that you are interested in collaborating with them.

Becoming a social media influencer is a fun way to live your life and garner the interest of those around you. You will slowly become a social media celebrity in your own right.

This chapter just provided a skeleton description of social media and the potential it has for your business. There are numerous advantages to using these various platforms, and it is in your best interest to see how they can benefit you in some way. Social media is a gold mine for marketing and generating extra income. The challenge comes in learning to use it properly.

Chapter 8

Accounting for Beginners

We will end this book by discussing a major logistical area of running a business: accounting. Without proper accounting, no matter how good or profitable your business is, it will not be financially well off because the money management portion of the business will not be taken care of properly. In this chapter, we will go over some of the basics of accounting. Even if you delegate this task to a professional or another business partner who is good with numbers, which we highly recommend, you should still have an idea of how accounting works. This way, you can make sure your finances are being managed properly.

The Basics of Accounting

Accounting for business is the in-depth process of recording, analyzing, and interpreting your business's financial information. Business owners must have a proper accounting foundation set up to meet all of the financial obligations and goals of their business. If you cannot master it, then you must outsource it to a trustworthy person. It is an aspect that cannot be ignored.

For proper accounting to occur within your business, you will need to have some specific forms and documents to showcase your business's financial health and performance. This will allow you to make better financial decisions that will help your business grow. People often ignore small expenses that are wasteful, but this is a mistake. Yes, there will be money lost during business practices. These are experiences that must be learned from and should not become normalized. The following are some documents to become aware of that provide valuable insight into your financial performance:

- An income statement: This document shows your company's profitability and how much your business has made or lost.
- A balance sheet: This will show your business's financial standing at a single point in time and the amount of money you've reinvested in your business.
- A profit and loss statement: This form showcases your income and expenses during a given period.
- A cash flow statement: This analyzes your business's financing, operating, and investing activities to show where and how you're receiving and spending money.
- A bank reconciliation form: This compares cash expenditures with your overall bank statements.

It's a good idea to get familiar with these documents. Even if you hire someone, your finances are still your responsibility. You never know when you'll need to know this information, so you should stay on top of it.

Proper Accounting Steps

As a business owner, you will be dealing with a lot of money going in and out. You must keep track of this money at all times. Getting behind, even for a little bit, can create headaches for you in the future. It is best to take some essential steps that will make it easier to keep track of your income and expenses. The following are some important steps to take for your accounting plan:

1. Open a business account that is completely separate from your other accounts. Use this account solely for business income and expenses and nothing else.

2. Itemize all of your expenses by departments. This way, you can see where all of your money is going and if the expenses are truly essential. And we do mean list every expense here.

3. Set up a proper payroll system. You can deduct employee pay, education expenses, and benefits from your taxes. This is why it's important to keep track of them through payroll. There are great software programs to help you with accounting, like Zenefits or Intuit QuickBooks Payroll.

4. Proper bookkeeping is crucial and should be done daily if possible. Keeping proper books allows you to keep a thumb on income, expenses, and overall business performance.

5. Identify the right payment methods for your needs. This will be how you receive money for your products and services. For a physical store, cash, credit card, and iPay are optimal methods. For online or distant businesses, credit card, PayPal, square, or other online payment methods will be useful. Consider the fees that these various platforms have.

6. Always review and evaluate your accounting methods to see if they're working for you. There are always updated methods and programs that are available, so keep abreast of those too.

The bottom line is that you need to pay close attention to your business's money flow, both in and out. Your business is how you create your livelihood, and you want to make sure you keep as much of your money as you can. Do not ignore the accounting aspect of your business, no matter how great your income is. Your business will not always be riding high, and this is where money management will really come into play.

Taxes

We have touched on taxes a little bit in this book, but they are so important that we wanted them to have their own section. We all have to pay taxes. All of the information we discussed in the previous section is essential for proper money management, but it is also valuable for making sure taxes are done properly. If you hire an accountant, they will likely be knowledgeable about taxes as well.

When you work for a company as an employee, your taxes are usually withheld with each paycheck. During tax season, you get a W2 form that summarizes your taxes and income for the previous year. You can then use an online program or go to a tax professional to file your taxes. When you own a business, you do not have this option. You need to be mindful of saving part of your net income and setting it aside for taxes. Many business owners will file their taxes quarterly to prevent having to make one big payment a year.

Your tax obligation will be dependent on many factors. Some of these include whether you have employees, if you collect sales tax, and how your legal structure is set up. Business taxes bring in a whole new set of laws and guidelines. A tax professional can help keep track of these rules and the many changes that come about every year. Tax laws do not stay the same. They are ever-changing.

Going Through an Audit

There is a myth that if you have someone else doing your taxes, they are responsible for answering to the IRS. Get this thought out of your head because it will not be that person who has to answer for your taxes. It's you. If the IRS has reason to believe that unethical practices are being done with tax preparation, you may end up going through an audit. This is another reason why keeping good records and following the rules is important. The following are some tips to avoid an audit:

- Do not try to expense entertainment events. For example, if you take a potential client to a ballgame, do it on your own dime, and do not put it as a business expense.

- Do not go overboard with deductions. Deduct what you are legally allowed to. This changes all the time, so having a tax professional to keep up with these changes will be beneficial. Trying to learn all of the tax laws while running your business is not practical.

- Incorporate your business or set up an LLC. This will show a higher level of organization, which will help keep you below the IRS's radar.

- Be proactive with changes. If your business suddenly grows, which requires more equipment and other expenses, then you may have to claim more deductions from one year to the next. This will be a huge red flag. What you can do is contact your local government ahead of time and showcase your new expenses with receipts. This will take extra work but can help prevent an audit.

- Avoid amended returns as much as possible. This means that you should make sure to do your taxes right the first time to prevent having to send a new return because of mistakes. These amended returns will also set off some red flags with the IRS. If you must do an amended return, so be it, but just do your best not to be in this position.

- File electronically, especially since there are so many options for doing so. Statistically, there is a 21% higher error rate with paper returns. This prompts the IRS to be wary of non-electronic returns (Conrad, 2019).

If you do end up getting audited, do not panic. Work with the IRS to get things settled as quickly as possible. Provide them with the information they need and be upfront about everything. Hopefully, you kept track of your expenses and income, as well as your receipts, in case they need them. Audits are never fun, but the easier you are to work with, the better off you will be.

Either learn the ins and outs of accounting and keep up with the new laws on a yearly basis or understand the basics of accounting and hire a trusted professional. This area is important so make sure the person you go with has an impeccable record. If one of your business partners will take care of the accounting portion, that's fine too. Just make sure you are aware of what's going on. The last thing you want is to be cheated unknowingly by a business partner.

Conclusion

We appreciate you reading our book, *Starting a Business Guide*. Our hope is that we gave you a lot of valuable information so that you are much more informed before you jump into the business world. Our intention with this book was not to deter you in any way. We encourage you to start a business that will be your passion and succeed in the long run. We just want to make sure you are informed as much as possible ahead of time.

Business has been the backbone of our society for generations. The entrepreneurial spirit is alive in many people, which is a great thing. Unfortunately, the recent problems, mainly due to the pandemic, have created more issues than anyone could have ever imagined. Many companies, especially small businesses, have received irrecoverable damages. Some were forced to close down permanently, which is a tragedy.

Fortunately, this gave rise to many other industries, including several online business opportunities. It takes a lot to succeed in business, and no matter what path you choose, there will be challenges along the way. It is best to be aware of them so you have a better chance of overcoming them. There are certain constants with every business idea and making sure that you start with a solid foundation is crucial to your success.

As we went through the chapters, we provided in-depth details about what a small business is and all that it entails. We also went over the challenges created by the recent pandemic and how to maintain or start a business afterward. The information provided in this section is not exclusive to the pandemic; it is relevant to any other problem that may arise. As a reminder, your business will go through many ups and downs, so being prepared is always essential.

Furthermore, we discussed how to set up a solid business plan, appropriate ways to invest in your business for optimal growth, and the importance of having an online presence even if you do not run an online business. Of course, online businesses, which surged forward after the pandemic hit, are great options for many people. They provide numerous advantages over traditional businesses that require a physical location.

Finally, this book covered the more forgotten but equally important aspects of running a business: accounting, marketing, analytics, and setting up a business plan. If you ignore these factors, your business will suffer immensely in the long run, and it might even shut down, as so many businesses do.

The next step is to take the information from this book and begin using it to create your dream business. A business must never be created on a whim, no matter how popular the idea is. Determine the problems you want to solve, do your research, set up the proper channels for success, and then move forward with faith. Your business will become an extension of you, so always put your best foot forward. We believe this book will provide a lot of beneficial information for the public. If you found this book to be valuable, then please help other people learn about it by leaving a review. Thank you for taking the time to read it.

References

A Better Lemonade Stand. (2019, October 28). *6 Social Media Platforms You Should Be Selling & Advertising On*. A Better Lemonade Stand. https://www.abetterlemonadestand.com/social-media-platforms-to-sell-on/

Advantages and Disadvantages of Instagram and How to Leverage Them. (2018, October 25). Burkhart Marketing.

http://burkhartmarketing.com/advantages-and-disadvantages-of-instagram-and-how-to-leverage-them/

Bluehost. (2016, November 1). *10 Small Businesses That Made It Big*. Official Bluehost Blog.

https://www.bluehost.com/blog/small-business/10-small-businesses-that-made-it-big-7527/

Boitnott, J. (2017, January 31). 10 Ways You Should Invest Your Company's First Profits. Entrepreneur.

https://www.entrepreneur.com/article/288456

Business Formation - Choose a Business Structure: LLC, Corporation, Sole Proprietorship, Partnership. (n.d.). LegalZoom.

https://www.legalzoom.com/business/business-formation/

Caster, Andrew. (2017, May 3). *Why Investments are Important for Your Business*. All Peers.

https://www.allpeers.com/investments-important-business/#:~:text=Most%20individuals%20know%20the%20impo rtance

Clement, J. *(2020, April 30). Facebook users worldwide 2020.* Statista.

https://www.statista.com/statistics/264810/number-of-monthly-active-facebook-users-worldwide/#:~:text=How%20many%20users%20does%20Faceboo k

Conrad, A. (2019, May 22). *6 Reasons Why Businesses Get Audited (and How to Avoid Them).* Blog.Capterra.Com.

https://blog.capterra.com/why-do-businesses-get-audited/

Coronavirus Relief for Small Businesses: Seven Ways to Get Help. (2020, May 5). GoFundMe.

https://www.gofundme.com/c/blog/coronavirus-relief-small-businesses

Decker, A. (2020, April 20). *Accounting 101: The Ultimate Guide to Accounting Basics.* Blog.Hubspot.Com.

https://blog.hubspot.com/sales/accounting-101

D'Angelo, M. (2019, January 30). *6 Things to Do Before Starting a Business*. Www.Businessnewsdaily.Com.

https://www.businessnewsdaily.com/1484-starting-a-business.htm

Famuyide, S. (n.d.). *Common Problems Faced by Business Analysts and Possible Solutions*. Business Analyst Learnings. https://businessanalystlearnings.com/blog/2013/4/29/common-problems-faced-by-business-analysts

Freedman, M. (2020, April 1). *Profitable Online Business Ideas*. Business News Daily.

https://www.businessnewsdaily.com/4572-online-business-ideas.html

Haden, J. (2018, July 20). *How to Write the Perfect Business Plan: A Comprehensive Guide*. Inc.Com; Inc.

https://www.inc.com/jeff-haden/how-to-write-perfect-business-plan-a-comprehensive-guide.html

How to Become an Influencer: 7 Steps to Becoming a Social Media Influencer. (2019, September 24). Influencer Marketing Hub.

https://influencermarketinghub.com/how-to-become-an-influencer/

McIntyre, G. (2017, May 10). *What Is the SBA's Definition of Small Business (And Why)?* Fundera Ledger; Fundera.

https://www.fundera.com/blog/sba-definition-of-small-business

Moeser, M. (2020, May 15). *How businesses are surviving the pandemic*. American Banker.

https://www.americanbanker.com/news/how-businesses-are-surviving-the-coronavirus-pandemic

Porter, J. (2013, January 15). *8 Ways to Come Up With a Business Idea*. Entrepreneur.

https://www.entrepreneur.com/slideshow/307451

Schroeder, B. (2020, April 9). *Startup Opportunities Coming Out Of The Pandemic—Some Are Opportunistic, Others Will Be Here For A Long Time*. Forbes.

https://www.forbes.com/sites/bernhardschroeder/2020/04/09/startup-opportunities-coming-out-of-the-pandemic-some-are-opportunistic-others-will-be-here-for-a-long-time/#134e36ce9350

S-Lawler, K. (2019, January 15). *Hallam*. Hallam.

https://www.hallaminternet.com/facebook-advertising-advantages-disadvantages/

Sikandar, M. (2017, November 8). *The 6 Biggest Business Problems for Small Business Owners | Statusbrew*. Social Media Marketing Insights | Statusbrew.

https://statusbrew.com/insights/small-business-problems-faced-by-small-business-owners/

Sun, C. (2016, March 7). *10 Mistakes to Avoid When Starting an Online Business*. Entrepreneur.

https://www.entrepreneur.com/article/250698

Suneson, G. (2020, March 21). *Industries hit hardest by coronavirus in the US include retail, transportation, and travel*. USA TODAY.

https://www.usatoday.com/story/money/2020/03/20/us-industries-being-devastated-by-the-coronavirus-travel-hotels-food/111431804/

Torry, H. (2020, April 1). Coronavirus Pandemic Widens Divide Between Online, Traditional Businesses. *Wall Street Journal*.

https://www.wsj.com/articles/coronavirus-pandemic-widens-divide-between-online-traditional-businesses-11585733402

What is Social Media Marketing? (2019). Buffer.Com. https://buffer.com/social-media-marketing#:~:text=Social%20media%20marketing%20is%20the

Why Investing In Your Business Is Important. (2016, September 12). Bluchic.

https://www.bluchic.com/why-investing-in-your-business-is-important/

Wilen, H. (2020, June 25). *How Five Small Businesses Have Survived the Covid-19 Pandemic.* Bizjournals.Com.

https://www.bizjournals.com/baltimore/news/2020/06/25/how-five-small-businesses-have-survived-covid-19.html

Wood, M. (2017, December 20). *6 Easy Ways to Raise Capital For Your Business.* Mycorporation; MyCorporation.

https://blog.mycorporation.com/2017/12/ready-to-expand-your-business-here-are-6-ways-to-raise-capital/